# BIBLE
# MAPBOOK

For Roey:
accurate navigator
on countless journeys

Copyright © 1985 Lion Publishing

Published by
**Lion Publishing plc**
Icknield Way, Tring, Herts, England
ISBN 0 85648 887 9
**Lion Publishing Corporation**
10885 Textile Road, Belleville, Michigan 48111, USA
ISBN 0 85648 887 9
**Albatross Books**
PO Box 320, Sutherland, NSW 2232, Australia
ISBN 0 86760 629 0

**Maps and artwork** Simon Jenkins
**Colour** Roy Lawrance and Lesley Passey

**British Library Cataloguing in Publication Data**

Jenkins, Simon
    Bible mapbook.—(A Lion book)
    1. Bible—Geography
    I. Title
    220.0′1    BS630
    ISBN 0-85648-887-9

**Library of Congress Cataloging in Publication Data**

Jenkins, Simon
    Bible mapbook.
    "A Lion book."
    Includes index.
    1. Bible—Geography—Maps.   I. Title.
G2230.J35 1985      912′.122      85–675090
ISBN 0–85648–887 9

First edition 1985
Printed in Italy

# BIBLE MAPBOOK

## SIMON JENKINS

A LION BOOK
Tring · Belleville · Sydney

# Bible Mapbook

# Introduction

The Bible is a book about real life. It tells us about a God who transcends our world, but who is also actively involved in it. This is why the Bible can point us to God by telling stories about what actually happened. The people of Israel treasured the stories of the parting of the Red Sea and the defeat of the Egyptians not out of nostalgia or simply because they enjoyed thrillers, but because these stories told them about the God who had saved them.

Many of the Bible's stories are packed with human detail. Who was the father of who, which side of the hill the town was on, how many days it took to get from A to B. The writers clearly knew their way around the country.

All this adds local variety and detail to the Bible's account, though for non-locals (most of us) it can be easy to get lost. Those of us who are foreigners to it all, who would not know whether to turn left or right to reach Bethlehem, need something of a guided tour to help us out.

This book aims to do that. By concentrating on a single event or idea per map it brings to life the significance and the excitement of what was happening. Seemingly obscure details that we thought got in the way of a good story now help to make the story tick as a real, human event.

Apart from the maps, the book also uses graphics generated by computer to give an accurate idea of the climbs and descents involved in some of the biblical accounts. These give an on-the-ground guide to journeys and battles that would be literally flat on an ordinary map.

The maps have been designed to be used alongside an open Bible. Bible passages are referred to in the text for each map, helping us to get over the bumps and around the corners of the story. The book proceeds in biblical book order and each chapter starts with an introduction to the period and details of the maps for the chapter.

Any book about the Bible will contain some traces of interpretation. This book is not intended to be a guide to all the points of view Christians take on Bible events. So, for example, alternative exodus routes are not discussed. *The Corinthian Affair* on page 116 is a probable interpretation of the evidence in the Bible. The depiction of Jericho on page 30, Samaria on page 63 and of the second temple on page 81 are impressions only.

*The Bible Mapbook* has been produced in the conviction that events described in the Bible matter. They are more than simply good stories; they point beyond themselves to God at work in our world. It is hoped that these maps will do their own work of pointing, too.

---

*Note*

Passages from the Bible are referred to in the following way:

# 1 Kings  19:1–18

**1 Kings** refers to the first of the two books of Kings

**19:1–18** means chapter 19, verses 1 to 18

# 1
# THE BIBLE'S WORLD

# Who Was Who?

**GREEKS**
The Greek Empire covered the East Mediterranean in the time between the Old and New Testaments. Greek (or Hellenistic) culture was the setting of the New Testament.

**ROMANS**
The Roman Empire was peaceful and organized in the time of the New Testament. It took over the Greek Empire.

**PHILISTINES**
Originally from the Aegean, settled here around the time of the exodus and conquest. Oppressed Israel during Judges, at war with Saul and David.

**EGYPTIANS**
The influential southern power of the Old Testament, although in steady decline.

■ Ancient city names
● Ancient names still in use
○ Modern city names

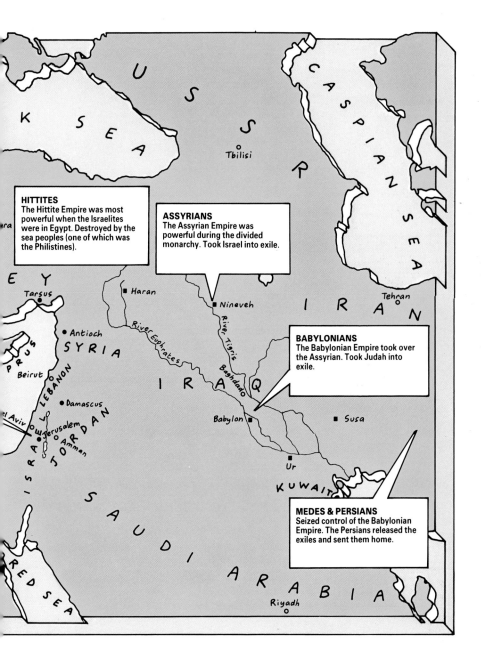

**HITTITES**
The Hittite Empire was most powerful when the Israelites were in Egypt. Destroyed by the sea peoples (one of which was the Philistines).

**ASSYRIANS**
The Assyrian Empire was powerful during the divided monarchy. Took Israel into exile.

**BABYLONIANS**
The Babylonian Empire took over the Assyrian. Took Judah into exile.

**MEDES & PERSIANS**
Seized control of the Babylonian Empire. The Persians released the exiles and sent them home.

# Israel: Old Testament

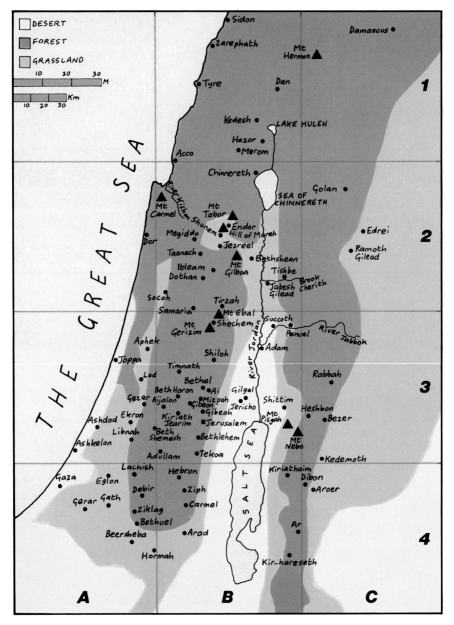

DESERT
FOREST
GRASSLAND

10  20  30 M
10  20  30 Km

Sidon
Zarephath
Damascus
Mt Hermon
Tyre
Dan
1
Kedesh
LAKE HULEH
Hazor
Merom
Acco
Chinnereth
SEA OF CHINNERETH
Golan
Mt Carmel
River Kishon
Mt Tabor
Shunem
Endor
Hill of Moreh
Megiddo
Jezreel
Edrei
2
Dor
Taanach
Mt Gilboa
Bethshean
Ramoth Gilead
Ibleam
Dothan
Tishbe
Jabesh Gilead
Brook Cherith
Socoh
Tirzah
Samaria
Mt Ebal
Shechem
Succoth
Mt Gerizim
Penuel
River Jabbok
Aphek
Adam
Joppa
Shiloh
Timnath
Lod
Bethel
Rabbah
3
Beth Horon
Ai
Gilgal
Gezer
Aijalon
Mizpah
Gibeon
Jericho
Shittim
Heshbon
Ekron
Gibeah
Mt Pisgah
Bezer
Ashdod
Kiriath Jearim
Jerusalem
Libnah
Beth Shemesh
Bethlehem
Mt Nebo
Ashkelon
Adullam
Tekoa
Kedemoth
Lachish
Hebron
Kiriathaim
Gaza
Eglon
Debir
Ziph
Dibon
Gerar
Gath
Carmel
Aroer
Ziklag
Bethuel
Ar
Beersheba
Arad
4
Hormah
Kir-hareseth

THE GREAT SEA

River Jordan

SALT SEA

A          B          C

# Israel: New Testament

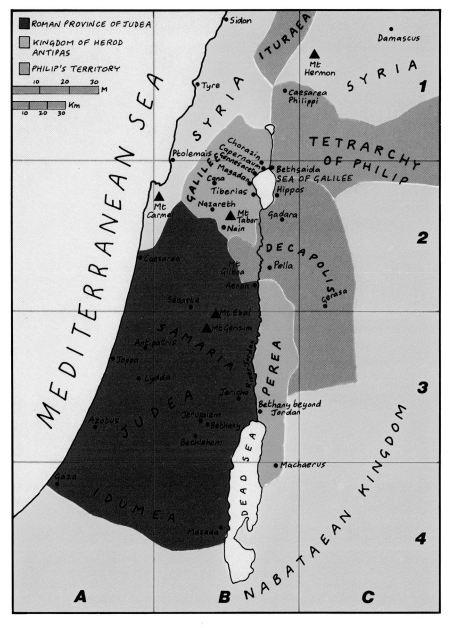

ROMAN PROVINCE OF JUDEA

KINGDOM OF HEROD ANTIPAS

PHILIP'S TERRITORY

10   20   30   M

10   20   30   Km

1

2

3

4

A

B

C

Sidon

Damascus

ITURAEA

Mt Hermon

Tyre

Caesarea Philippi

SYRIA

SYRIA

S Y R I A

MEDITERRANEAN SEA

Ptolemais

GALILEE

Chorazin
Capernaum
Gennesaret
Magadan
Cana
Tiberias
Nazareth

Bethsaida
SEA OF GALILEE
Hippos

TETRARCHY OF PHILIP

Mt Carmel

Mt Tabor
Nain

Gadara

DECAPOLIS

Caesarea

Mt Gilboa

Pella

Gerasa

Aenon

Sebaste

Mt Ebal
Mt Gerizim

Antipatris

SAMARIA

Joppa

Lydda

PEREA

River Jordan

Jericho

JUDEA

Azotus

Jerusalem
Bethany

Bethany beyond Jordan

Bethlehem

DEAD SEA

Gaza

IDUMEA

Machaerus

NABATAEAN KINGDOM

Masada

# The Land Bridge

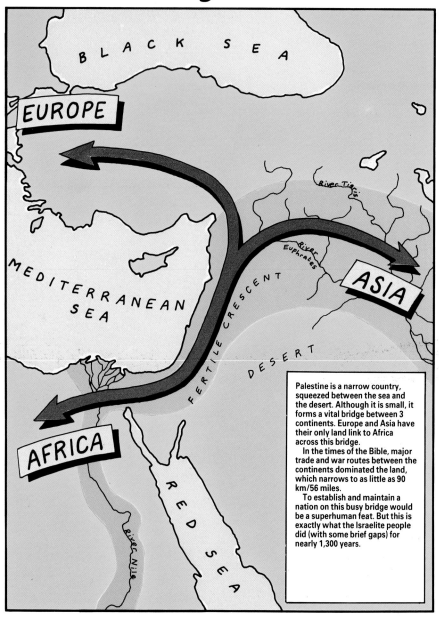

Palestine is a narrow country, squeezed between the sea and the desert. Although it is small, it forms a vital bridge between 3 continents. Europe and Asia have their only land link to Africa across this bridge.

In the times of the Bible, major trade and war routes between the continents dominated the land, which narrows to as little as 90 km/56 miles.

To establish and maintain a nation on this busy bridge would be a superhuman feat. But this is exactly what the Israelite people did (with some brief gaps) for nearly 1,300 years.

# Road Routes

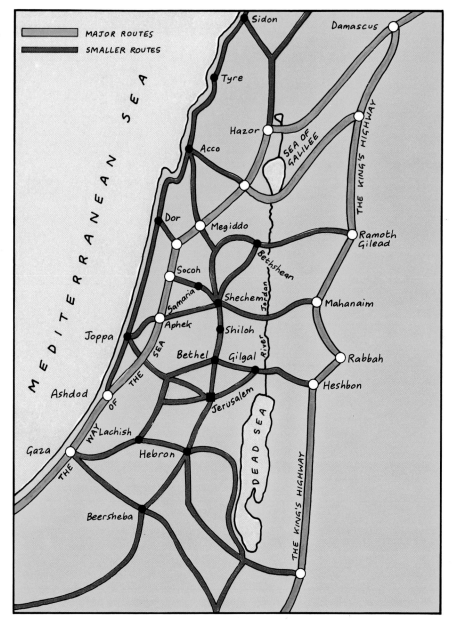

# The Shape of the Land

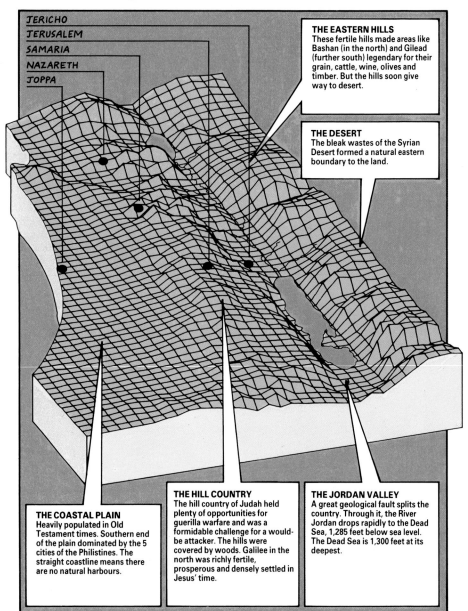

JERICHO
JERUSALEM
SAMARIA
NAZARETH
JOPPA

**THE EASTERN HILLS**
These fertile hills made areas like Bashan (in the north) and Gilead (further south) legendary for their grain, cattle, wine, olives and timber. But the hills soon give way to desert.

**THE DESERT**
The bleak wastes of the Syrian Desert formed a natural eastern boundary to the land.

**THE COASTAL PLAIN**
Heavily populated in Old Testament times. Southern end of the plain dominated by the 5 cities of the Philistines. The straight coastline means there are no natural harbours.

**THE HILL COUNTRY**
The hill country of Judah held plenty of opportunities for guerilla warfare and was a formidable challenge for a would-be attacker. The hills were covered by woods. Galilee in the north was richly fertile, prosperous and densely settled in Jesus' time.

**THE JORDAN VALLEY**
A great geological fault splits the country. Through it, the River Jordan drops rapidly to the Dead Sea, 1,285 feet below sea level. The Dead Sea is 1,300 feet at its deepest.

# 2

# ABRAHAM'S PEOPLE

The story of the nation of Israel begins with one man, Abram (later called Abraham), who lived 2,000 years before Jesus Christ. Answering a call of God, he emerged from an obscure past in Mesopotamia and travelled to Canaan. But he brought more than just his suitcase. With him were flocks, herds, servants, animal-minders, his family and the tents they all camped in.

God promised Abram that he would have many descendants – and that they would not always be nomads. The land of Canaan would become their home to occupy and enjoy. They would finally roll up their tents, build houses and settle as a nation.

# Abraham's People

**Maps appearing in this chapter are:**

● **Father of a Nation** (page 19). Abram and his entourage travel to Canaan, around 1900 BC. His children are promised the land to live in, but Abram himself continues a life of wandering.
● **Abram Saves Lot** (page 20). Abram rescues Lot, who has been kidnapped by invading armies.
● **Jacob Comes Home** (page 21). Jacob is Abram's grandson. He returns from self-imposed exile to Canaan, where he brings up his twelve sons and one daughter.
● **Joseph's Story** (page 22). Joseph, second youngest of Jacob's sons, is hated by his brothers for his boasting. They sell him to slave traders bound for Egypt. But the roles are reversed when Joseph becomes governor of Egypt during a famine. . .
● **Into Slavery** (page 23). Abraham's children had been promised a land of their own. But 600 years after Abraham they are slaves to the Egyptian people.
● **Exit from Egypt** (page 24). The Israelites are dramatically freed from slavery under the leadership of Moses around 1270 BC. They receive God's law on Mt Sinai.
● **Moses Defeats Sihon and Og** (page 26). For forty years the Israelites wander in the desert as punishment for grumbling against God. Finally they approach Canaan, the Promised Land.

❝I am going to give you so many descendants that no one will be able to count them all; it would be as easy to count all the specks of dust on earth!❞
God's promise to Abraham

❝I have come down to rescue my people from the hand of the Egyptians and to bring them up out of that land into a good and spacious land, a land flowing with milk and honey. . .❞
God calls Moses

❝I will sing to the Lord for he is highly exalted. The horse and its rider he has hurled into the sea.❞
Moses' song (after the defeat of the Egyptians in the sea)

❝Why did you bring us out of Egypt into this miserable place where nothing will grow? There's no corn, no figs, no grapes, no pomegranates. There is not even any water to drink!❞
The Israelites complain in the desert

❝There has never been a prophet in Israel like Moses; the Lord spoke with him face to face.❞
When Moses died

# Father of a Nation

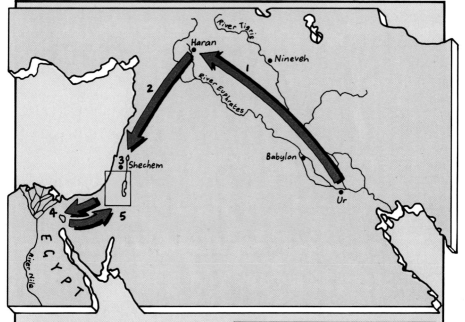

Abram (later called Abraham) is called by God to travel to Canaan.

**1**  Abram's father Terah takes his family to go to Canaan from Ur. Settle in Haran.

**2**  Terah dies. Abram called by God to go on to Canaan. He travels with his wife Sarai, nephew Lot, flocks of sheep and his workmen. God promises Abram many descendants, to become a nation used by God.

**3**  In Canaan, Abram builds altars to the Lord at Shechem and near Bethel. God identifies this as the land for Abram's descendants.

**4**  Famine forces Abram to live for a while in Egypt.

**5**  They return to Canaan. Lack of good animal pasture leads to arguments between Abram's and Lot's men. They decide to separate.

**6**  (Small map) Lot chooses the fertile Jordan Valley, leaving Abram with the hill country.

**7**  God renews his promise to Abram, who builds an altar at Hebron.

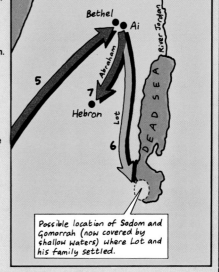

Possible location of Sodom and Gomorrah (now covered by shallow waters) where Lot and his family settled.

# Abram Saves Lot

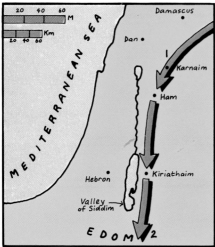

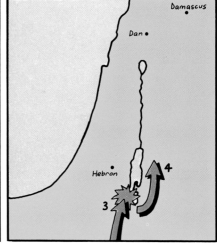

1  Four local kings in the Valley of Siddim rebel against their distant overlords in Babylonia and Elam. The overlords (five kings) travel south to restore their rule, defeating other peoples on the way.
2  They carry out raids into the mountains of Edom.

3  The five kings defeat the four rebel kings.
4  They carry off people and loot from Sodom and Gomorrah, including Lot, Abram's nephew.

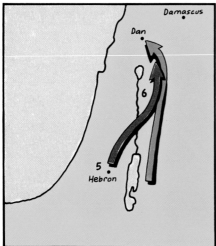

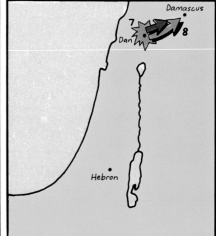

5  Abram hears that Lot has been captured.
6  He pursues the kings along the King's Highway north to Dan.

7  Abram's men attack the enemy by night and defeat them.
8  They pursue the fleeing armies, rescue Lot and recover the other prisoners.

# Jacob Comes Home

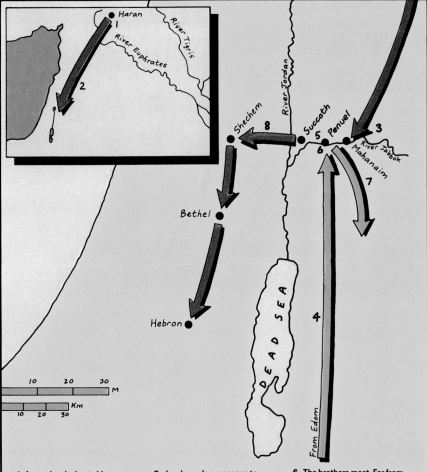

**1 Inset** Jacob cheats his brother Esau of their father's blessing. Esau plans to kill him, so Jacob flees to Haran. There he works for his uncle Laban, who in turn cheats Jacob.
**2** After 20 years, Jacob secretly takes his wives, children, servants and flocks back to Canaan. Laban pursues, but they reach an agreement.

**3** Jacob sends a message to Esau, telling him of his return.
**4** But Esau is already on his way to Jacob with 400 men. Frightened, Jacob sends large gifts on ahead to Esau.
**5** The night before they meet, Jacob wrestles with God. He is told: 'You have struggled with God and with men, and you have won; so your name will be Israel.'

**6** The brothers meet. Far from being angry, Esau runs to his brother and welcomes him with great affection.
**7** Esau returns to Edom. Jacob promises to follow him.
**8** But instead, Jacob goes on into Canaan.

# Joseph's Story

Joseph, sold by his brothers into slavery in Egypt, has now become governor in charge of food stored against the coming famine.

1   Jacob their father sends 10 of Joseph's brothers to Egypt for grain. He keeps the youngest son Benjamin (his favourite) with him for safety.

2   They do not recognize Joseph and he pretends not to know them. He accuses them of spying. He keeps Simeon hostage, sends the rest home with food. They must bring back Benjamin to prove they are not spies.

3   On the way home they are frightened to find money in the top of their sacks.

4   Jacob is unwilling to let Benjamin go – he has already lost Joseph and Simeon. He changes his mind only when the famine threatens starvation.

River Nile

Hebron

Heliopolis

Memphis

M   60   40   20
Km   60   40   20

5   The 9 brothers and Benjamin go to Egypt, loaded down with gifts for Joseph.

6   Simeon is released and Joseph gives a great feast.

7   He sends them home again with food. But he orders his silver cup to be planted in Benjamin's sack.

8   A servant pursues them and discovers Joseph's cup.

9   Joseph says they can go free, but Benjamin will stay as his slave. Judah pleads with Joseph on behalf of Jacob. With great emotion, Joseph tells them who he is.

10   The 11 brothers return to Jacob. He comes to live in Egypt.

River Nile

Hebron

Heliopolis

Memphis

B   BENJAMIN

S   SIMEON

THE OTHER BROTHERS

# Into Slavery

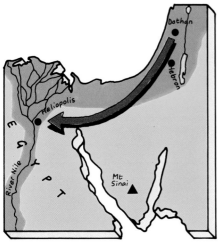

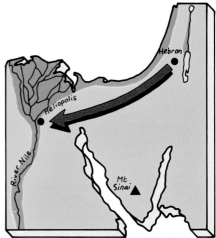

Joseph is one of Jacob's 12 sons. His older brothers grow to hate him for his arrogance. Jacob sends Joseph to Dothan where the brothers are looking after the sheep. They decide to kill him but on second thoughts sell him to traders. Joseph is taken to Egypt. (Genesis 37:12–36)

Years later, Joseph has become a governor in Egypt, in charge of food. Famine strikes and Joseph's brothers travel to Egypt to buy corn. Joseph recognizes them and eventually tells them who he is. Jacob and his family move down into Egypt. (Genesis 42–47:12)

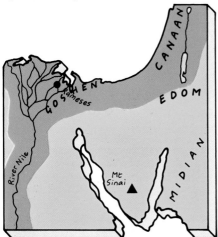

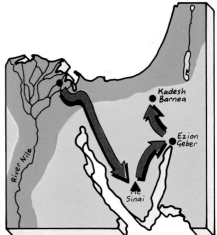

After 430 years, the Hebrew descendants of Jacob's family have become slaves to the Egyptians, used on their building projects. They live in Goshen. God raises up Moses and Aaron his brother to liberate the Hebrews. But the king refuses to let the people leave. (Exodus 1–5:21)

A series of disasters strike Egypt, but still the king remains stubborn. At last the Hebrews are allowed to leave, but even then the Egyptians pursue them, only to be defeated. They travel to Mt Sinai, where Moses receives the Law from God. (Exodus 6:28–20:17)

# Exit from Egypt

**1** Israelites told to leave Egypt by Pharaoh Ramesses II. The years of slavery are over (Exodus 12:29–36).

**2** They travel to the region of the Bitter Lakes (Exodus 12:37–39; 13:17–14:4).

**3** Ramesses changes his mind and pursues his escaped slaves. He traps the Israelites against the sea (Exodus 14:5–12).

**4** God tells Moses to hold out his stick over the sea. The waters are driven back and the people cross on dry land. Egyptians drowned as the water returns (Exodus 14:13–31).

**5** After 3 days they arrive at Marah – but water is too bitter to drink (Exodus 15:22–26).

**6** God first provides manna and quails to eat (Exodus 16).

**7** God provides water from rock. The Amalekites attack and are defeated. Moses' father-in-law advises Moses (Exodus 17–18).

**8** At Mt Sinai, Israel receives the Law from God (Exodus 19–32).

**9** Miriam becomes leprous for her jealousy and rebellion against Moses (Numbers 12:1–16).

**10** Eleven days after leaving Mt Sinai, Moses sends 12 spies into Canaan (Numbers 13:1–24).

**11** The spies return. Ten bring bad reports, leading the people to rebellion. They want a new leader to take them back to Egypt (Numbers 13:25–14:10).

**12** As punishment, God sends them to wander in the desert 40 years before entering Canaan (Numbers 14:11–38).

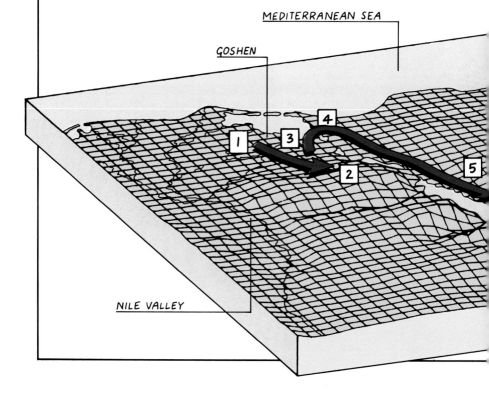

MEDITERRANEAN SEA

GOSHEN

NILE VALLEY

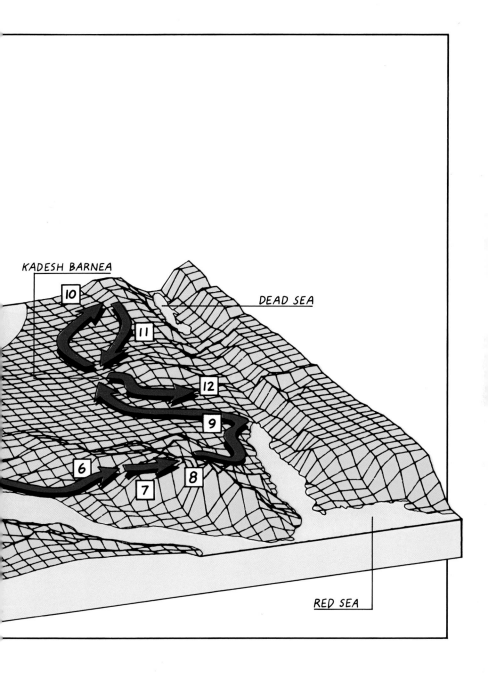

# Moses Defeats Sihon and Og

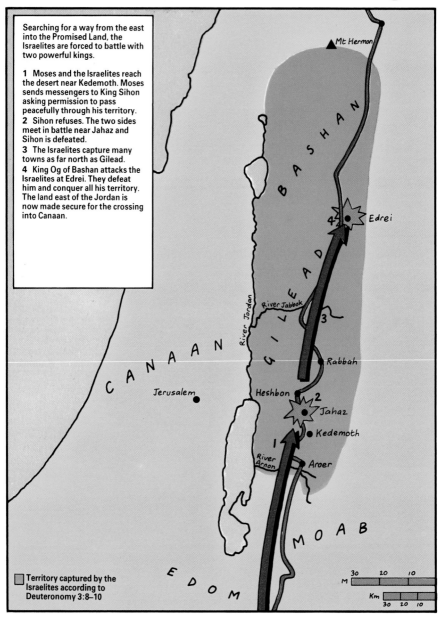

Searching for a way from the east into the Promised Land, the Israelites are forced to battle with two powerful kings.

**1** Moses and the Israelites reach the desert near Kedemoth. Moses sends messengers to King Sihon asking permission to pass peacefully through his territory.

**2** Sihon refuses. The two sides meet in battle near Jahaz and Sihon is defeated.

**3** The Israelites capture many towns as far north as Gilead.

**4** King Og of Bashan attacks the Israelites at Edrei. They defeat him and conquer all his territory. The land east of the Jordan is now made secure for the crossing into Canaan.

Territory captured by the Israelites according to Deuteronomy 3:8–10

# 3

# LAND OF
# MILK AND HONEY

Before crossing over the River Jordan into Canaan, the people of
Israel were a nation looking for somewhere to happen. Like
Abraham, they still lived a nomadic life in tents. But their large
numbers threatened nations already established in the region.
Their arrival on the doorstep of Canaan provoked terror and
hostility among the people living there.

  Joshua, who became leader after Moses had died, led his
people to conquer and settle the land. But the conquest was not
complete, and this led to troubled times. The people of Israel
were tempted to worship the old gods of Canaan, and they were
attacked again and again by enemies they had wounded but not
defeated. The Promised Land became a violent land. Israel's
leaders in these times were called 'judges'.

# Land of Milk and Honey

**Maps appearing in this chapter are:**

● **Over the Jordan** (page 29).
Miraculous signs continue to accompany
the nation's birth. The people cross the
River Jordan on dry ground at about
1230 BC.
● **Defeat by Decibels** (page 30). After
careful spying out and a strange method
of attack, Jericho is taken. This gives the
Israelites a good foothold in the country.
● **Attack on Ai** (page 31). Another city
falls. The Israelites learn that victory is
not automatic – it depends on their
obedience to God.
● **Gibeon Rescued** (page 32). After
tricking Joshua into making a treaty with
them, the people of Gibeon are attacked
by their Canaanite neighbours. Joshua
rescues them.
● **Joshua's Campaigns** (page 33).
Joshua wages war from north to south,
giving Israel a precarious hold over the
land.
● **Fixing the Boundaries** (page 34). The
twelve tribes of Israel (descended from

Jacob's twelve sons) are now given their
promised share of the land.
● **Cities of Refuge** (page 35). Six cities
are designated as places of sanctuary for
fugitives escaping rough justice.
● **Philistine Sea Raiders** (page 36). The
Philistines quickly establish themselves
as Israel's bitterest enemies. Who were
they – and where had they come from?
● **Israel Surrounded** (page 37). The
time of the judges sees Israel under the
attack or the rule of many strong nations.
● **Deborah's Victory** (page 38).
Deborah and Barak, two of Israel's
judges, end a cruel regime with a
devastating victory in battle.
● **Gideon's Night Raid** (page 39).
Another judge, Gideon, defeats the
Midianites with a shock attack by night.
● **The Ark Captured!** (page 40). The
Ark of God, containing the tablets of the
law, is captured by the Philistines in
battle. But this great prize of war is
returned voluntarily. . .

**❝I know that the Lord has given you
this land. Everyone in the country is
terrified of you. ❞**
Rahab, prostitute of Jericho, to the two
Israeli spies she sheltered in her home

**❝Any one of you can make a
thousand men run away, because the
Lord your God is fighting for you, just
as he promised. ❞**
Joshua

**❝But if serving the Lord seems
undesirable to you, then choose for**

**yourselves this day whom you will
serve, whether the gods your
forefathers served beyond the River,
or the gods of the Amorites, in whose
land you are living. But as for me and
my household, we will serve the Lord. ❞**
Joshua's final speech

**❝Separate everyone who laps up the
water with his tongue like a dog, from
everyone who gets down on his knees
to drink. ❞**
Gideon narrows his troops down to 300

# Over the Jordan

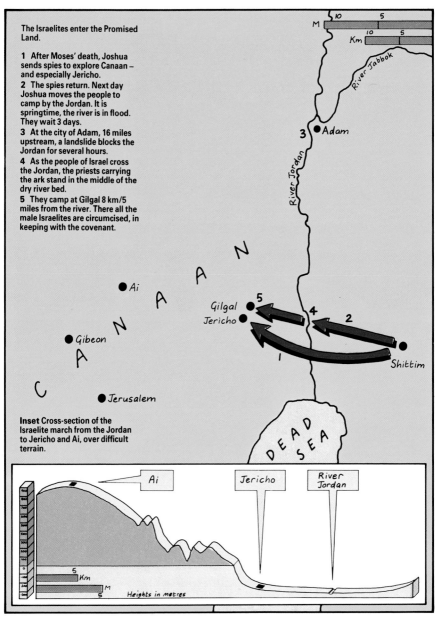

The Israelites enter the Promised Land.

**1** After Moses' death, Joshua sends spies to explore Canaan – and especially Jericho.

**2** The spies return. Next day Joshua moves the people to camp by the Jordan. It is springtime, the river is in flood. They wait 3 days.

**3** At the city of Adam, 16 miles upstream, a landslide blocks the Jordan for several hours.

**4** As the people of Israel cross the Jordan, the priests carrying the ark stand in the middle of the dry river bed.

**5** They camp at Gilgal 8 km/5 miles from the river. There all the male Israelites are circumcised, in keeping with the covenant.

**Inset** Cross-section of the Israelite march from the Jordan to Jericho and Ai, over difficult terrain.

Heights in metres

# Defeat by Decibels

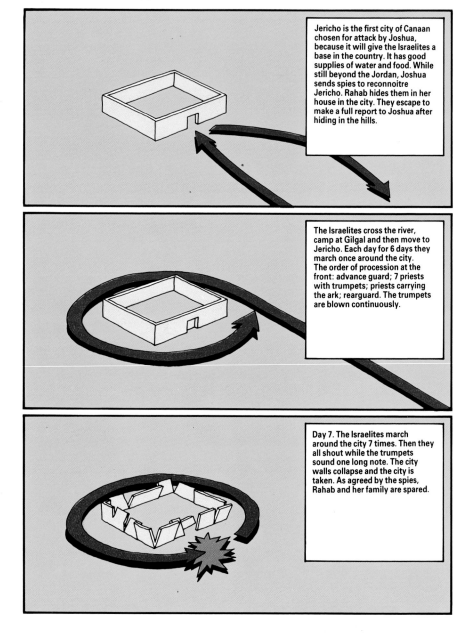

Jericho is the first city of Canaan chosen for attack by Joshua, because it will give the Israelites a base in the country. It has good supplies of water and food. While still beyond the Jordan, Joshua sends spies to reconnoitre Jericho. Rahab hides them in her house in the city. They escape to make a full report to Joshua after hiding in the hills.

The Israelites cross the river, camp at Gilgal and then move to Jericho. Each day for 6 days they march once around the city. The order of procession at the front: advance guard; 7 priests with trumpets; priests carrying the ark; rearguard. The trumpets are blown continuously.

Day 7. The Israelites march around the city 7 times. Then they all shout while the trumpets sound one long note. The city walls collapse and the city is taken. As agreed by the spies, Rahab and her family are spared.

# Attack on Ai

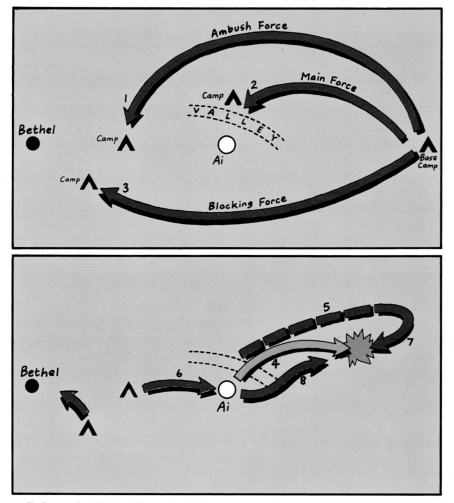

The first attack on Ai had ended in defeat for Israel because of one man's sin. But now, because of their obedience, God had promised victory. . .

1 Joshua sends out an ambush force at night to hide on the far side of Ai.
2 Next morning Joshua leads the main force to camp opposite the gate of Ai.
3 A third force is sent out to hide between Ai and Bethel, to block any intervention (Joshua 8:12).
4 The king of Ai leads his men out.
5 Joshua's main force pretends to retreat. The men of Ai pursue, as in the previous battle.

6 The ambush force enters unprotected Ai and sets it on fire.
7 Joshua's force turns to attack the men of Ai.
8 The ambush force joins the battle and overcomes the enemy.

# Gibeon Rescued

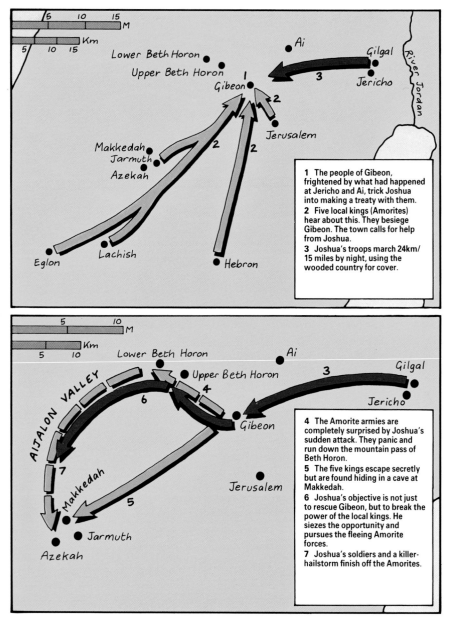

**1** The people of Gibeon, frightened by what had happened at Jericho and Ai, trick Joshua into making a treaty with them.
**2** Five local kings (Amorites) hear about this. They besiege Gibeon. The town calls for help from Joshua.
**3** Joshua's troops march 24km/15 miles by night, using the wooded country for cover.

**4** The Amorite armies are completely surprised by Joshua's sudden attack. They panic and run down the mountain pass of Beth Horon.
**5** The five kings escape secretly but are found hiding in a cave at Makkedah.
**6** Joshua's objective is not just to rescue Gibeon, but to break the power of the local kings. He siezes the opportunity and pursues the fleeing Amorite forces.
**7** Joshua's soldiers and a killer-hailstorm finish off the Amorites.

# Joshua's Campaigns

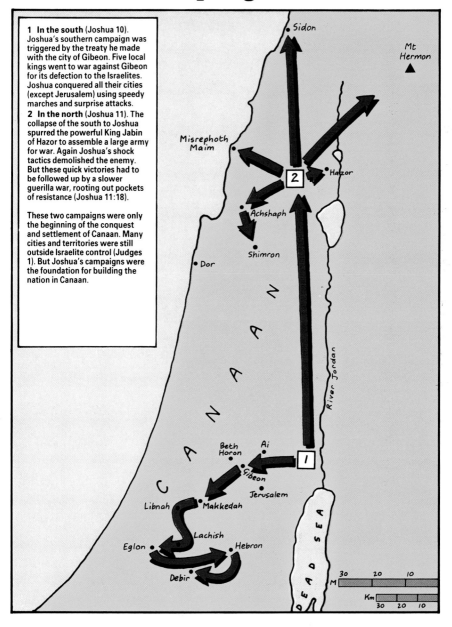

**1 In the south** (Joshua 10). Joshua's southern campaign was triggered by the treaty he made with the city of Gibeon. Five local kings went to war against Gibeon for its defection to the Israelites. Joshua conquered all their cities (except Jerusalem) using speedy marches and surprise attacks.

**2 In the north** (Joshua 11). The collapse of the south to Joshua spurred the powerful King Jabin of Hazor to assemble a large army for war. Again Joshua's shock tactics demolished the enemy. But these quick victories had to be followed up by a slower guerilla war, rooting out pockets of resistance (Joshua 11:18).

These two campaigns were only the beginning of the conquest and settlement of Canaan. Many cities and territories were still outside Israelite control (Judges 1). But Joshua's campaigns were the foundation for building the nation in Canaan.

Sidon

Mt Hermon

Misrephoth Maim

Hazor

2

Achshaph

Shimron

Dor

C A N A A N

River Jordan

Beth Horon

Ai

Gibeon

Jerusalem

1

Libnah

Makkedah

Lachish

Eglon

Hebron

Debir

DEAD SEA

30   20   10
M

Km
30   20   10

# Fixing the Boundaries

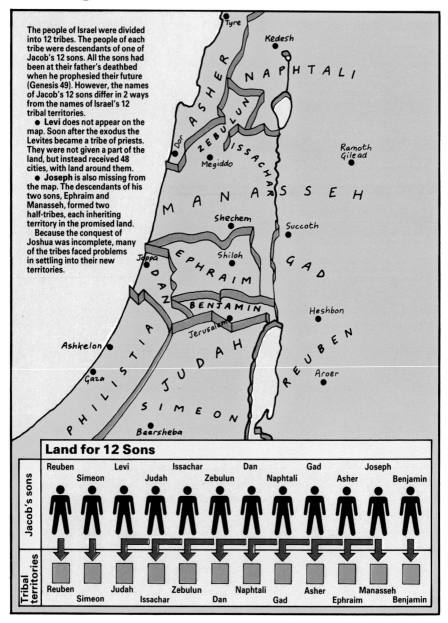

The people of Israel were divided into 12 tribes. The people of each tribe were descendants of one of Jacob's 12 sons. All the sons had been at their father's deathbed when he prophesied their future (Genesis 49). However, the names of Jacob's 12 sons differ in 2 ways from the names of Israel's 12 tribal territories.

● **Levi** does not appear on the map. Soon after the exodus the Levites became a tribe of priests. They were not given a part of the land, but instead received 48 cities, with land around them.

● **Joseph** is also missing from the map. The descendants of his two sons, Ephraim and Manasseh, formed two half-tribes, each inheriting territory in the promised land.

Because the conquest of Joshua was incomplete, many of the tribes faced problems in settling into their new territories.

### Land for 12 Sons

| | | | | |
|---|---|---|---|---|
| Jacob's sons | Reuben / Simeon | Levi / Judah | Issachar / Zebulun | Dan / Naphtali | Gad / Asher | Joseph / Benjamin |
| Tribal territories | Reuben / Simeon | Judah / Issachar | Zebulun / Dan | Naphtali / Gad | Asher / Ephraim | Manasseh / Benjamin |

# Cities of Refuge

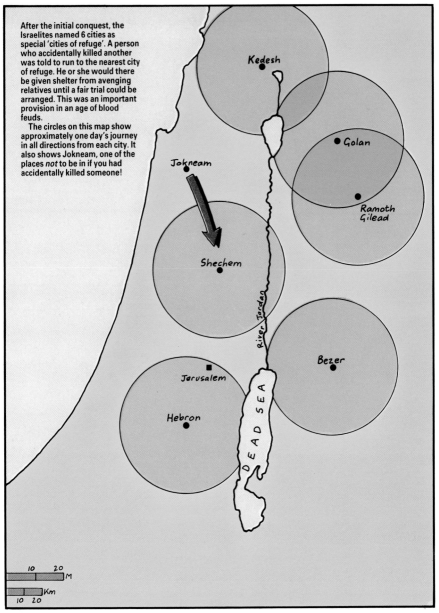

After the initial conquest, the Israelites named 6 cities as special 'cities of refuge'. A person who accidentally killed another was told to run to the nearest city of refuge. He or she would there be given shelter from avenging relatives until a fair trial could be arranged. This was an important provision in an age of blood feuds.

The circles on this map show approximately one day's journey in all directions from each city. It also shows Jokneam, one of the places *not* to be in if you had accidentally killed someone!

Kedesh

Golan

Jokneam

Ramoth Gilead

Shechem

River Jordan

Bezer

Jerusalem

Hebron

DEAD SEA

10   20
M

Km
10   20

# Philistine Sea Raiders

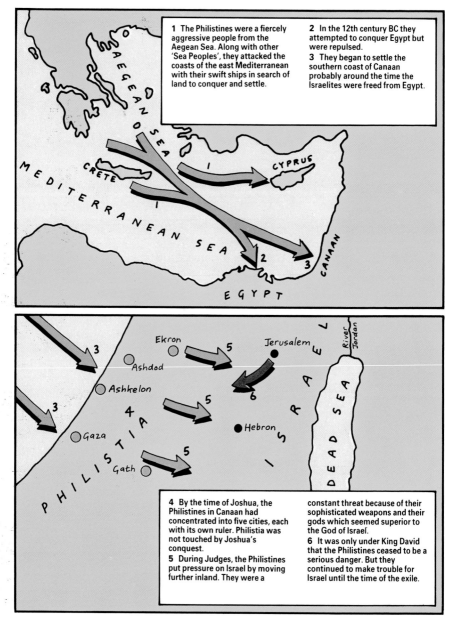

1  The Philistines were a fiercely aggressive people from the Aegean Sea. Along with other 'Sea Peoples', they attacked the coasts of the east Mediterranean with their swift ships in search of land to conquer and settle.

2  In the 12th century BC they attempted to conquer Egypt but were repulsed.

3  They began to settle the southern coast of Canaan probably around the time the Israelites were freed from Egypt.

4  By the time of Joshua, the Philistines in Canaan had concentrated into five cities, each with its own ruler. Philistia was not touched by Joshua's conquest.

5  During Judges, the Philistines put pressure on Israel by moving further inland. They were a constant threat because of their sophisticated weapons and their gods which seemed superior to the God of Israel.

6  It was only under King David that the Philistines ceased to be a serious danger. But they continued to make trouble for Israel until the time of the exile.

# Israel Surrounded

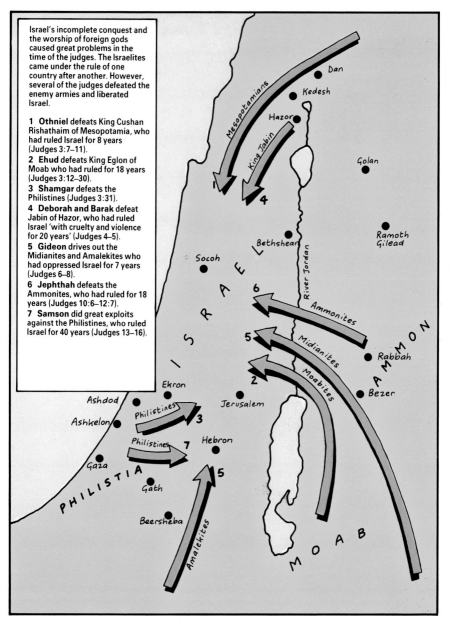

Israel's incomplete conquest and the worship of foreign gods caused great problems in the time of the judges. The Israelites came under the rule of one country after another. However, several of the judges defeated the enemy armies and liberated Israel.

**1  Othniel** defeats King Cushan Rishathaim of Mesopotamia, who had ruled Israel for 8 years (Judges 3:7–11).
**2  Ehud** defeats King Eglon of Moab who had ruled for 18 years (Judges 3:12–30).
**3  Shamgar** defeats the Philistines (Judges 3:31).
**4  Deborah and Barak** defeat Jabin of Hazor, who had ruled Israel 'with cruelty and violence for 20 years' (Judges 4–5).
**5  Gideon** drives out the Midianites and Amalekites who had oppressed Israel for 7 years (Judges 6–8).
**6  Jephthah** defeats the Ammonites, who had ruled for 18 years (Judges 10:6–12:7).
**7  Samson** did great exploits against the Philistines, who ruled Israel for 40 years (Judges 13–16).

# Deborah's Victory

Israel had been oppressed by the violent rule of King Jabin of Hazor for 20 years. Deborah, a prophet, made plans with Barak to lure the army of Jabin to defeat. . .

**1** Deborah and Barak gather an army from some of the tribes to Mt Tabor, dominating the area.

**2** Sisera, commander of Jabin's army, brings his troops and 900 iron chariots to the foot of Tabor.

**3** Deborah gives the signal to attack (possibly after a heavy rainstorm). Barak's forces sweep down the steep slopes of Mt Tabor. Sisera's troops panic and head towards the marshy River Kishon.

**4** The rainstorm floods the river. Sisera's chariots are useless or are swept away (Judges 5:21). His army is routed.

**5** Local Canaanite kings try to aid Sisera's men by Taanach, but they too are defeated (Judges 5:19).

**6** Barak pursues the retreating army as far as Harosheth. It is completely defeated.

**7** Sisera himself abandons his now-useless chariot. He flees for his life, but is killed while sleeping in a tent.

# Gideon's Night Raid

The Midianites, fierce desert people who used camels in their attacks, had ruled over Israel for 7 years.

1 A Midianite army camps in the Valley of Jezreel.
2 Gideon calls the northern tribes of Israel to his home town, Ophrah.
3 The Israelite force moves to the Spring of Harod. Gideon narrows his troops down to 300 men.

4 At night, Gideon and his servant spy out the Midianite camp. Gideon then divides his army into 3 groups. Each man holds a trumpet and a torch hidden in a jar. They surprise the Midianites by blowing their trumpets and smashing the jars at the edges of the camp.
5 Confused, the Midianites flee towards the Jordan Valley. Extra troops pursue and defeat them completely.

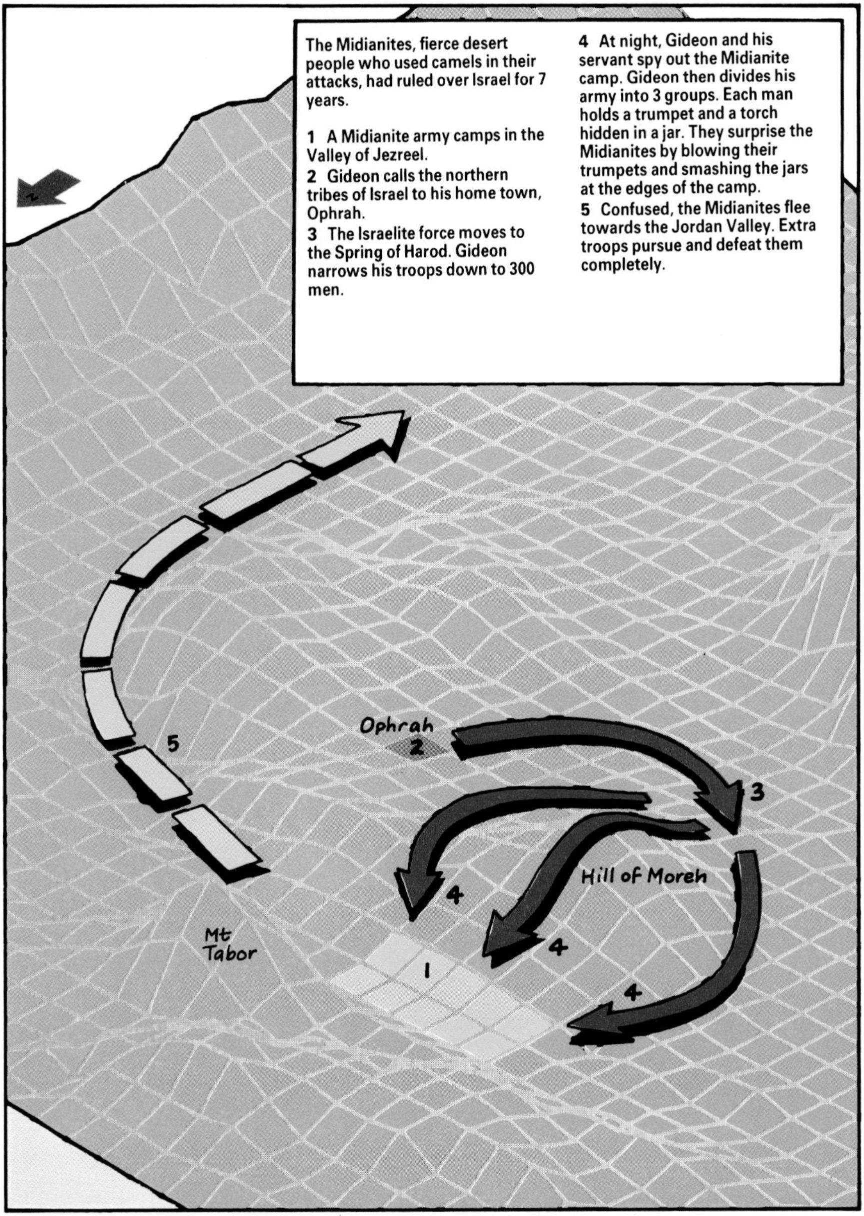

Ophrah
2

5

3

Hill of Moreh

4

4

Mt Tabor

1

4

# The Ark Captured!

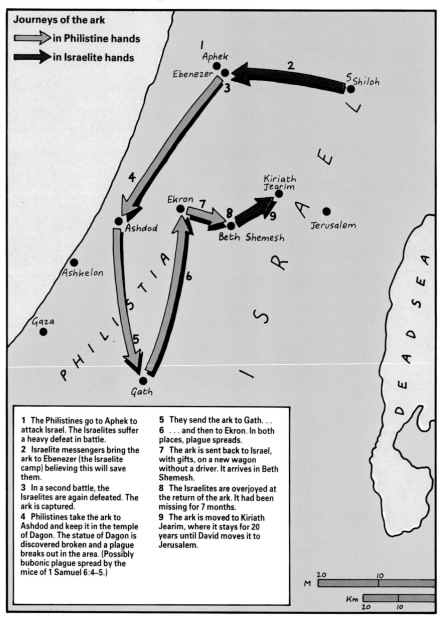

Journeys of the ark

⟹ in Philistine hands

➤ in Israelite hands

1 Aphek

Ebenezer

2

3

Shiloh

4

Kiriath Jearim

Ekron 7

8

9

Ashdod

Jerusalem

Beth Shemesh

Ashkelon

6

Gaza

5

Gath

PHILISTIA

ISRAEL

DEAD SEA

1 The Philistines go to Aphek to attack Israel. The Israelites suffer a heavy defeat in battle.

2 Israelite messengers bring the ark to Ebenezer (the Israelite camp) believing this will save them.

3 In a second battle, the Israelites are again defeated. The ark is captured.

4 Philistines take the ark to Ashdod and keep it in the temple of Dagon. The statue of Dagon is discovered broken and a plague breaks out in the area. (Possibly bubonic plague spread by the mice of 1 Samuel 6:4–5.)

5 They send the ark to Gath. . .

6 . . . and then to Ekron. In both places, plague spreads.

7 The ark is sent back to Israel, with gifts, on a new wagon without a driver. It arrives in Beth Shemesh.

8 The Israelites are overjoyed at the return of the ark. It had been missing for 7 months.

9 The ark is moved to Kiriath Jearim, where it stays for 20 years until David moves it to Jerusalem.

20                    10

M

Km

20        10

# 4

# GIVE US
# A KING!

Israel's experience of terror and oppression in the time of the judges led many people to a burning desire for a king, 'like the other nations', who would defeat their enemies decisively. Saul, Israel's first king, was a failure. But under David and Solomon, the kingdom became secure and wealthy.

But the kings came with a price tag. Many of them were corrupt leaders who led Israel away from its faith in God. Under the kings a division between rich and poor developed. These defects emerged from the very first days of Israel's new rulers.

# Give Us a King!

**Maps appearing in this chapter are:**

● **Saul's Donkey Search** (page 43). The prophet Samuel anoints Saul as Israel's first king in 1050 BC.

● **Philistine Havoc** (page 44). Saul is soon put to the test by a Philistine invasion. Under pressure he disobeys God. Samuel tells him he will be replaced as king.

● **Jonathan's Risk** (page 45). In the end it is Saul's son, Jonathan, who precipitates the Philistines' defeat.

● **While the King Slept. . .** (page 46). Meanwhile, David has been secretly anointed king to follow Saul. The king becomes obsessed at killing David and hunts him down. But David proves his loyalty.

● **Saul's Final Battle** (page 47). Saul's dismal end occurs during a disastrous Philistine invasion in 1010 BC. David becomes king.

● **Jerusalem Captured** (page 48). David conquers the Jebusites at Jerusalem and makes the city his capital.

● **Crippling the Philistines** (page 49). The Philistines, after years of threatening Israel, are routed by David.

● **David Subdues his Enemies** (page 50). With a series of military campaigns, David makes the frontiers of his kingdom secure.

● **Uriah's Death Warrant** (page 51). Intoxicated by the power of kingship, David has one of his soldiers killed and steals his wife. This stirs up a swarm of violence later in his reign.

● **Revolt Against David** (page 52). Absalom, David's son, leads a rebellion and is killed in the attempt.

● **Solomon: Wheeler-Dealer** (page 53). Solomon was the successor to David's kingdom, crowned in 971BC. His business acumen and wisdom made him internationally famous.

● **Paying Solomon's Bills** (page 54). However, Solomon's court was supported by the taxation of Israel.

● **Solomon's Women** (page 55). Solomon was also legendary for his wives and mistresses, who led him far from God.

**❝ We want a king over us. Then we will be like all the other nations, with a king to lead us and to go out before us and fight our battles. ❞**
The people demand a king

**❝ Saul has slain his thousands, and David his tens of thousands. ❞**
A popular chant that turned Saul against David

**❝ I lie down and sleep;
I wake again, because the Lord sustains me.
I will not fear the tens of thousands drawn up against me on every side. ❞**
A psalm of David, when he fled from Absalom

**❝ Take the impurities out of silver and the artist can produce a thing of beauty. Keep evil advisers away from the king and his government will be known for its justice. ❞**
A proverb, said to be by Solomon

# Saul's Donkey Search

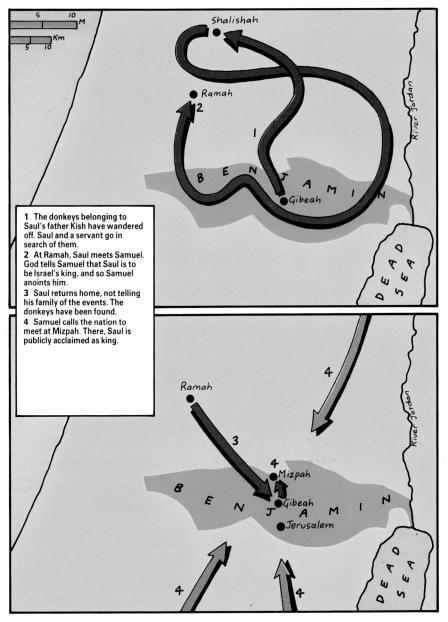

1 The donkeys belonging to Saul's father Kish have wandered off. Saul and a servant go in search of them.
2 At Ramah, Saul meets Samuel. God tells Samuel that Saul is to be Israel's king, and so Samuel anoints him.
3 Saul returns home, not telling his family of the events. The donkeys have been found.
4 Samuel calls the nation to meet at Mizpah. There, Saul is publicly acclaimed as king.

# Philistine Havoc

Saul had been made king to rid Israel of the Philistines. His chance to do this soon came.
**1** Saul sets up camp in Michmash with 3,000 men.
**2** He sends 1,000 men under his son Jonathan to attack the Philistine fortress of Gibeah. Jonathan kills the Philistine commander of the area.
**3** Saul goes to Gilgal and calls Israel to war.

**4** The Philistines, threatened by Jonathan's action, move with a large force to Michmash. Saul's troops begin to desert him.
**5** Samuel had instructed Saul to wait for him before taking action. After 7 days, Saul offers sacrifices, hoping to reunite his

men. Samuel is angry and predicts Saul's downfall.
**6** Saul joins Jonathan at Gibeah. His troops have declined to 600.
**7** Saul and Jonathan camp at Geba, opposite the Philistines.
**8** The Philistines raid the area.
**9** Twenty Philistine soldiers block the head of the Michmash canyon against attack.

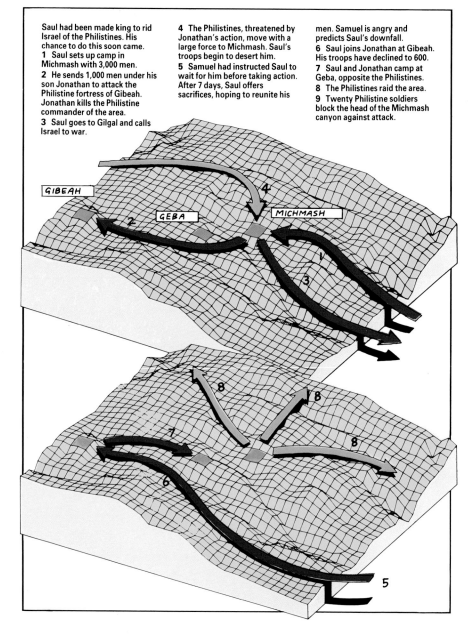

# Jonathan's Risk

1 Saul's troops move up to Migron. Both sides wait for each other to move.
2 While the Philistines watch the troops at Migron for any signs of activity, Jonathan and his weapon carrier secretly leave the camp. Not even Saul knows.

3 They creep up through the Michmash canyon, surprise the 20 Philistine soldiers and kill them.
4 Panic spreads through the Philistine camp.

5 Saul seizes the advantage and attacks.
6 The Philistines flee, pursued by Saul.
7 Some of the Israelite deserters come out of hiding to join in the attack.

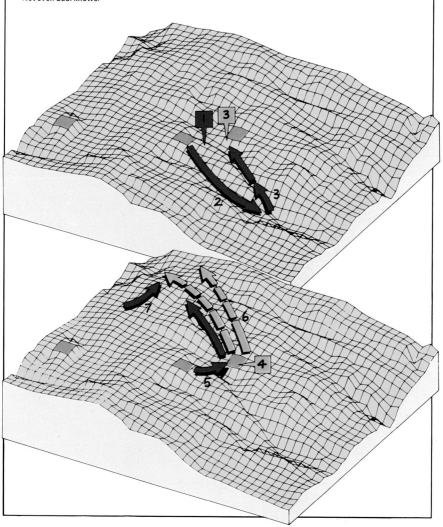

# While the King Slept...

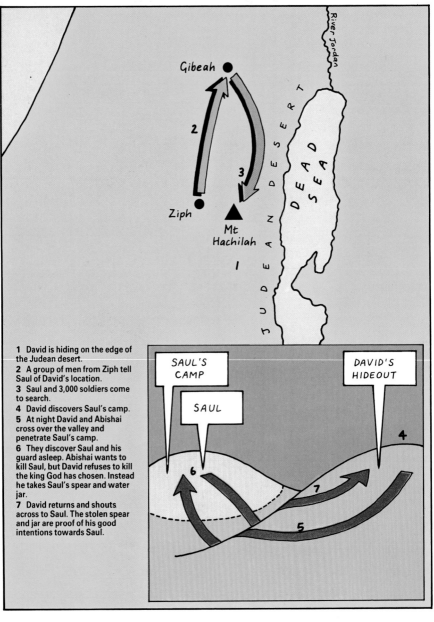

1  David is hiding on the edge of the Judean desert.
2  A group of men from Ziph tell Saul of David's location.
3  Saul and 3,000 soldiers come to search.
4  David discovers Saul's camp.
5  At night David and Abishai cross over the valley and penetrate Saul's camp.
6  They discover Saul and his guard asleep. Abishai wants to kill Saul, but David refuses to kill the king God has chosen. Instead he takes Saul's spear and water jar.
7  David returns and shouts across to Saul. The stolen spear and jar are proof of his good intentions towards Saul.

# Saul's Final Battle

1  The Philistine armies march up the coastal plain and then turn into the Valley of Jezreel, camping at Shunem. They plan an attack into the heart of Israel.

2  Saul's troops camp on Mt Gilboa – a good defensive position.

3  Saul is terrified at the size of the Philistine army. He is unable to get any guidance from God about what to do.

4  Despite his own prohibition of mediums and fortune tellers in Israel, Saul goes by night to consult a medium in Endor. She foretells disaster.

5  The Philistines attack Mt Gilboa. The Israelites are put to flight. Saul kills himself, and his son Jonathan is also killed. David sings a lament for Saul and Jonathan (2 Samuel 1:17–27).

# Jerusalem Captured

David had been king for over 7 years, ruling from Hebron. But he needed a new capital. Jerusalem was still in foreign hands, occupied by the Jebusites. It held a good defensive position, surrounded on 4 sides by valleys, and had a good source of water.

**1** David besieges the city, probably from the north, the weakest point in its defences.

**2** The Jebusites defy David to capture the city. They had made an underground tunnel to the Gihon spring, outside the city walls, closing up the natural approach to the spring.

**3 Inset** David promises that the first of his men to kill a Jebusite will be made commander of his army. Joab breaks into the water tunnel (possibly through its natural approach).

**4 Inset** Joab and his men take the city by surprise and it falls to David. David rules from Jerusalem for 33 years.

1 Chronicles 11:4–9

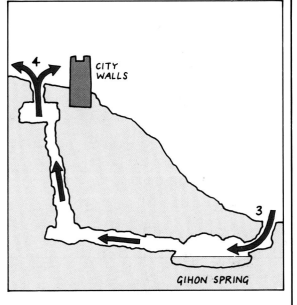

CITY WALLS

GIHON SPRING

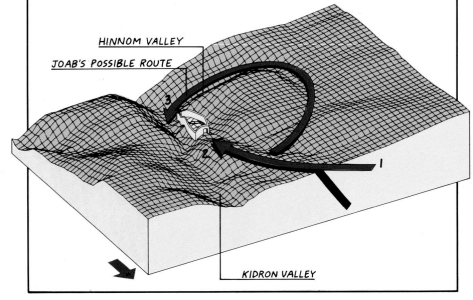

HINNOM VALLEY

JOAB'S POSSIBLE ROUTE

KIDRON VALLEY

# Crippling the Philistines

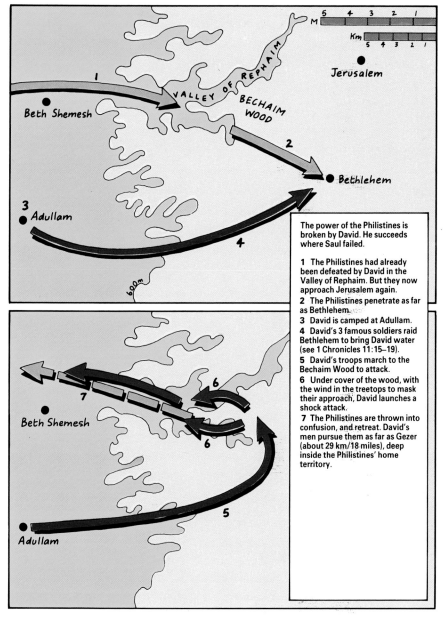

The power of the Philistines is broken by David. He succeeds where Saul failed.

**1** The Philistines had already been defeated by David in the Valley of Rephaim. But they now approach Jerusalem again.

**2** The Philistines penetrate as far as Bethlehem.

**3** David is camped at Adullam.

**4** David's 3 famous soldiers raid Bethlehem to bring David water (see 1 Chronicles 11:15–19).

**5** David's troops march to the Bechaim Wood to attack.

**6** Under cover of the wood, with the wind in the treetops to mask their approach, David launches a shock attack.

**7** The Philistines are thrown into confusion, and retreat. David's men pursue them as far as Gezer (about 29 km/18 miles), deep inside the Philistines' home territory.

# David Subdues his Enemies

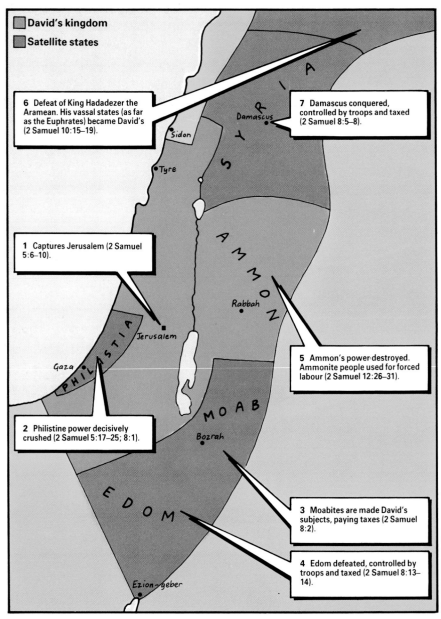

David's kingdom

Satellite states

**6** Defeat of King Hadadezer the Aramean. His vassal states (as far as the Euphrates) became David's (2 Samuel 10:15–19).

**7** Damascus conquered, controlled by troops and taxed (2 Samuel 8:5–8).

**1** Captures Jerusalem (2 Samuel 5:6–10).

**5** Ammon's power destroyed. Ammonite people used for forced labour (2 Samuel 12:26–31).

**2** Philistine power decisively crushed (2 Samuel 5:17–25; 8:1).

**3** Moabites are made David's subjects, paying taxes (2 Samuel 8:2).

**4** Edom defeated, controlled by troops and taxed (2 Samuel 8:13–14).

Damascus

Sidon

Tyre

SYRIA

AMMON

Rabbah

Jerusalem

Gaza

PHILISTIA

MOAB

Bozrah

EDOM

Ezion-geber

# Uriah's Death Warrant

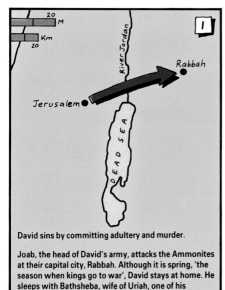

**1**

David sins by committing adultery and murder.

Joab, the head of David's army, attacks the Ammonites at their capital city, Rabbah. Although it is spring, 'the season when kings go to war', David stays at home. He sleeps with Bathsheba, wife of Uriah, one of his soldiers. She becomes pregnant.

**2**

David calls Uriah home from the siege of Rabbah. He tries to make him go home to be with Bathsheba. But Uriah, out of loyalty to his comrades, refuses. David sends him back to Joab with a letter. It is his own death warrant.

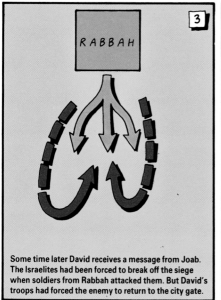

**3**

Some time later David receives a message from Joab. The Israelites had been forced to break off the siege when soldiers from Rabbah attacked them. But David's troops had forced the enemy to return to the city gate.

**4**

One group of Israelite soldiers had fought too close to the city wall and were killed by arrows. Uriah (who had been placed in the front line) was one of them. David sends a message back to Joab: 'Don't be upset. You never can tell who will die in battle.' David marries Bathsheba. He thinks his problems are over.

# Revolt Against David

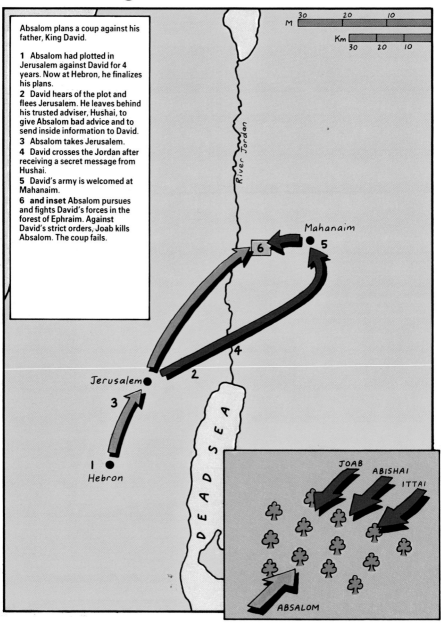

Absalom plans a coup against his father, King David.

**1** Absalom had plotted in Jerusalem against David for 4 years. Now at Hebron, he finalizes his plans.

**2** David hears of the plot and flees Jerusalem. He leaves behind his trusted adviser, Hushai, to give Absalom bad advice and to send inside information to David.

**3** Absalom takes Jerusalem.

**4** David crosses the Jordan after receiving a secret message from Hushai.

**5** David's army is welcomed at Mahanaim.

**6 and inset** Absalom pursues and fights David's forces in the forest of Ephraim. Against David's strict orders, Joab kills Absalom. The coup fails.

# Solomon: Wheeler-Dealer

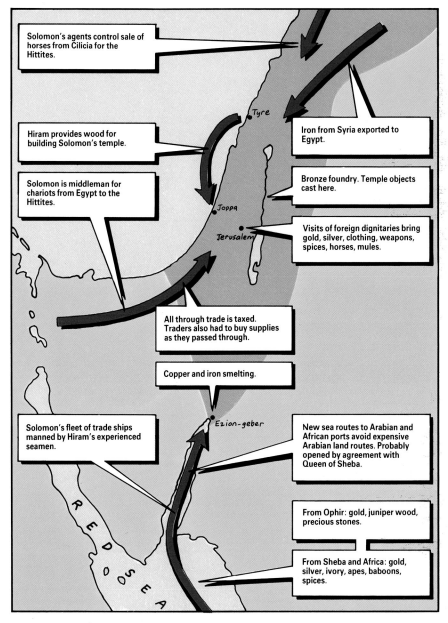

Solomon's agents control sale of horses from Cilicia for the Hittites.

Hiram provides wood for building Solomon's temple.

Solomon is middleman for chariots from Egypt to the Hittites.

Iron from Syria exported to Egypt.

Bronze foundry. Temple objects cast here.

Visits of foreign dignitaries bring gold, silver, clothing, weapons, spices, horses, mules.

All through trade is taxed. Traders also had to buy supplies as they passed through.

Copper and iron smelting.

Solomon's fleet of trade ships manned by Hiram's experienced seamen.

New sea routes to Arabian and African ports avoid expensive Arabian land routes. Probably opened by agreement with Queen of Sheba.

From Ophir: gold, juniper wood, precious stones.

From Sheba and Africa: gold, silver, ivory, apes, baboons, spices.

Tyre

Joppa

Jerusalem

Ezion-geber

RED SEA

# Paying Solomon's Bills

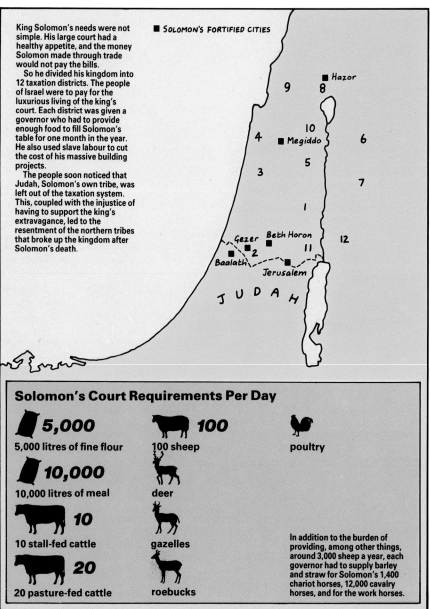

King Solomon's needs were not simple. His large court had a healthy appetite, and the money Solomon made through trade would not pay the bills.

So he divided his kingdom into 12 taxation districts. The people of Israel were to pay for the luxurious living of the king's court. Each district was given a governor who had to provide enough food to fill Solomon's table for one month in the year. He also used slave labour to cut the cost of his massive building projects.

The people soon noticed that Judah, Solomon's own tribe, was left out of the taxation system. This, coupled with the injustice of having to support the king's extravagance, led to the resentment of the northern tribes that broke up the kingdom after Solomon's death.

■ SOLOMON'S FORTIFIED CITIES

9   8   ■ Hazor

10
4   ■ Megiddo   6

3   5

7

1

Gezer   Beth Horon
■   ■         12
2   11

Baalath
Jerusalem

J U D A H

## Solomon's Court Requirements Per Day

**5,000**
5,000 litres of fine flour

**100**
100 sheep

poultry

**10,000**
10,000 litres of meal

deer

**10**
10 stall-fed cattle

gazelles

**20**
20 pasture-fed cattle

roebucks

In addition to the burden of providing, among other things, around 3,000 sheep a year, each governor had to supply barley and straw for Solomon's 1,400 chariot horses, 12,000 cavalry horses, and for the work horses.

# Solomon's Women

Solomon married the king of Egypt's daughter. Her father gave her the city of Gezer as a wedding present. Solomon built a special wing of the palace for her.

According to 1 Kings 11:3, 'Solomon married 700 princesses and also had 300 concubines.' Oriental kings married in this way to strengthen political and trading relations with foreign countries. The sheer number of women who passed through the royal bedroom shows the confidence and economic success of Solomon's reign.

However, there was a price to pay. The foreign wives brought with them alien gods – and they expected Solomon to allow these gods a place in his kingdom. By the time he was old, Solomon had betrayed Israel's faith in the one God. He built places to worship Molech, god of Ammon, and Chemosh, god of Moab on the Mt of Offence (as it was later known), east of Jerusalem. He also began to worship Astarte, goddess of Sidon. Solomon's places of worship were later destroyed by King Josiah.

# 5

# THE TWO KINGDOMS

There had been tension between northerners and southerners in Israel for some time, but after the death of Solomon in 930 BC north and south were ripped apart. The division was never healed. The southern kingdom (Judah) continued under the rule of David's descendants, while the northern kingdom (Israel) had a less stable monarchy, subject to coups, assassinations and palace intrigues.

The two kingdoms continued alongside each other for 210 years, sometimes at war, but also during periods of peace and prosperity. Prophets arose in both Israel and Judah, warning that God's judgement would fall because each nation was betraying its faith in God. For Israel this judgement came in 722 BC. Assyria, one of the great powers of the time, invaded and took the people into exile, never to return.

# The Two Kingdoms

**Maps appearing in this chapter are:**

❝My father scourged you with whips;
I will scourge you with scorpions.❞
King Rehoboam's harsh words
precipitate the division

❝How long will you waver between
two opinions? If the Lord is God, follow
him; but if Baal is God, follow him.❞
Elijah challenges the people on Mt
Carmel

❝Go to the Lord, and you will live. If
you do not go, he will sweep down like
fire on the people of Israel. The fire
will burn up the people of Bethel, and
no one will be able to put it out. You are
doomed, you that twist justice and
cheat people out of their rights!❞
Amos, prophet to Israel

# The Great Divide

Solomon's kingdom is broken in two.

**1** Jeroboam, an official of Solomon's (in charge of slave labour), is met by a prophet. He is told that he will become ruler of the 10 northern tribes.

**2** Jeroboam either plans a coup against Solomon, or is suspected of it. Solomon tries to kill him, and he flees to Egypt.

**3** Solomon dies. His son Rehoboam travels to Shechem to be proclaimed king.

**4** Jeroboam arrives in Shechem and leads a northern revolt against Rehoboam.

**5** Rehoboam sends a messenger to Jeroboam, but he is stoned to death. Rehoboam runs for his life back to Jerusalem. He plans for war against the northern tribes, but never attempts it.

**6 Inset** The northern tribes become Israel; the southern tribes, Judah.

30   20   10
M

Km
30   20   10

M A N A S S E H

Shechem

E P H R A I M

River Jordan

4

3

5

1

Jerusalem

2

To Egypt

DEAD SEA

ISRAEL

Samaria

Jerusalem

JUDAH

JEROBOAM

REHOBOAM

# Elijah on the Run

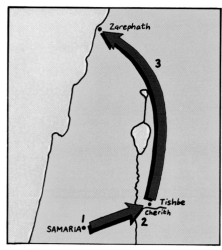

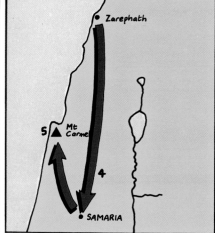

1   Elijah prophesies to King Ahab a 3 year drought in Israel.

2   Elijah hides at the brook of Cherith.

3   When the brook dries up he goes to Zarephath. He stays 3 years with a widow and her son.

4   Elijah goes to Ahab and tells him to gather the people of Israel and the prophets of Baal on Mt Carmel.

5   On Carmel, the Lord proves that he alone is God by sending down fire on Elijah's sacrifice. 450 prophets of Baal are put to death.

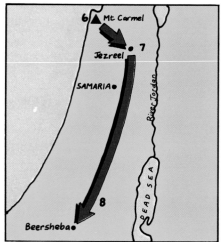

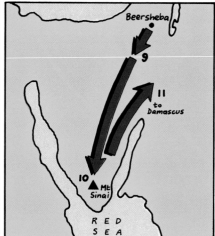

6   The drought ends with a great storm.

7   Elijah returns to Jezreel. There Ahab's wife Jezebel vows immediate revenge for the death of her prophets.

8   Elijah runs for his life, leaving his servant at Beersheba.

9   He journeys for a day into the desert. Depressed and weak, he is strengthened for the journey to Mt Sinai.

10   At Sinai Elijah receives a vision of God.

11   Elijah is sent to Damascus to appoint Elisha as his successor.

# Ahab and the Stray Arrow

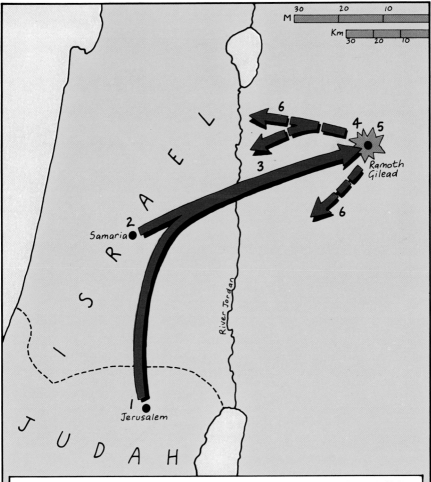

King Benhadad of Syria had promised to return the northern territory of Gilead to Israelite rule (1 Kings 20:34). But he had not done this.

**1** Jehoshaphat of Judah goes to Samaria to urge Ahab of Israel to join him in attacking the Syrians at Ramoth Gilead.

**2** Ahab consults his court prophets. All predict success, except for Micaiah, who has a reputation for bad news. He tells Ahab that his army will soon be scattered, without a leader.

**3** Ahab throws Micaiah into prison until his safe return, and then heads for battle alongside Jehoshaphat.

**4** During the battle, 32 chariots have orders to seek out and kill Ahab. They fail to find him, but a stray arrow finds a gap in Ahab's armour and fatally wounds him.

**5** Ahab pulls back from the front line. But he stays in the battle, to reassure his soldiers.

**6** At sunset, Ahab dies and his army is scattered, as predicted by Micaiah.

# Naaman is Healed

**1** Naaman, commander of the Syrian army, gets leprosy. He hears from his Israelite servant girl about Elisha's healing powers.

**2** The king of Syria sends Naaman to Samaria. He goes to Elisha's house.

**3** Elisha instructs Naaman to wash in the River Jordan 7 times. Naaman feels insulted, but his servants persuade him. He is cured.

**4** Naaman returns to Elisha, to give him a gift. Elisha refuses and sends him home.

**5** But Gehazi, Elisha's servant, follows Naaman and tells him Elisha would like 3,000 pieces of silver. Naaman insists on 6,000 pieces. On Gehazi's return home, Elisha uncovers his deception and Gehazi is stricken with leprosy.

Damascus

SYRIA

ISRAEL

Samaria

River Jordan

Jerusalem

JUDAH

DEAD SEA

M   30   20   10

Km   30   20   10

# Deserted Siege Camp

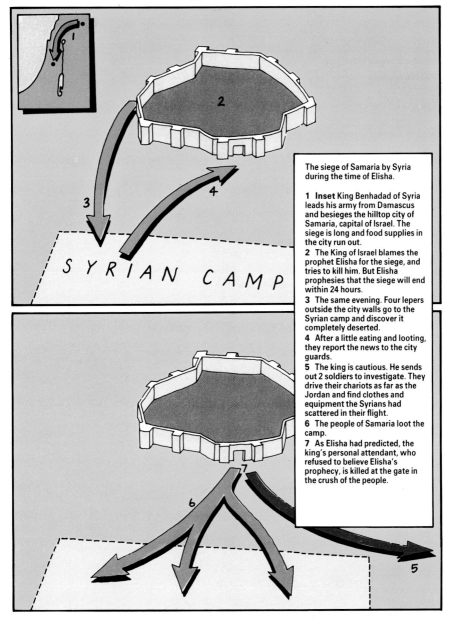

The siege of Samaria by Syria during the time of Elisha.

**1  Inset** King Benhadad of Syria leads his army from Damascus and besieges the hilltop city of Samaria, capital of Israel. The siege is long and food supplies in the city run out.

**2** The King of Israel blames the prophet Elisha for the siege, and tries to kill him. But Elisha prophesies that the siege will end within 24 hours.

**3** The same evening. Four lepers outside the city walls go to the Syrian camp and discover it completely deserted.

**4** After a little eating and looting, they report the news to the city guards.

**5** The king is cautious. He sends out 2 soldiers to investigate. They drive their chariots as far as the Jordan and find clothes and equipment the Syrians had scattered in their flight.

**6** The people of Samaria loot the camp.

**7** As Elisha had predicted, the king's personal attendant, who refused to believe Elisha's prophecy, is killed at the gate in the crush of the people.

SYRIAN CAMP

# The Superpowers Move In

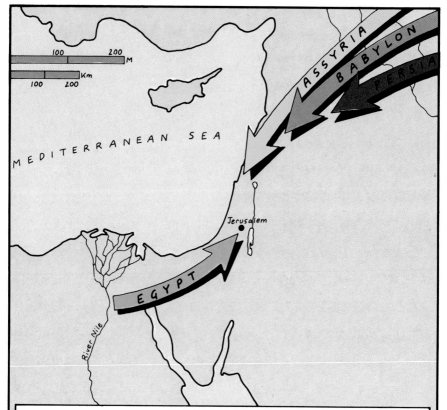

During the period of the Old Testament, 4 superpowers turned their unwelcome attention on Palestine:

**1** **Egypt**  The great southern power in the Old Testament, Egypt was in gradual decline. This was occasionally halted by a number of powerful kings, some of whom invaded Palestine and challenged the northern superpowers. Judah and Israel were often tempted to form alliances with Egypt against the north.

**2** **Assyria**  The Assyrians were the first of a succession of empires that swallowed up parts of Palestine. They exiled Israel and subdued Judah. Their empire collapsed when Nineveh fell to the Babylonians in 612BC.

**3** **Babylon**  The Babylonian Empire took over where the Assyrians left off. They took Judah into exile and successfully invaded Egypt. But their power was eroded by a series of weak rulers. In 539BC Cyrus the Persian took over the empire with little opposition.

**4** **Persia**  The Persian Empire was larger than its two predecessors. It was also more humane in returning exiles (Judah among them) to their homelands. The Persian empire was overrun by Alexander the Great around 331BC.

Alexander's Greek Empire was followed by the Roman Empire of New Testament times.

# Land-hungry Empires

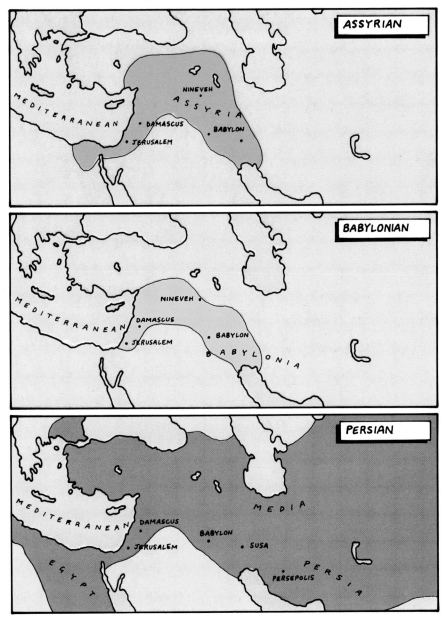

# Ahaz Calls Assyria

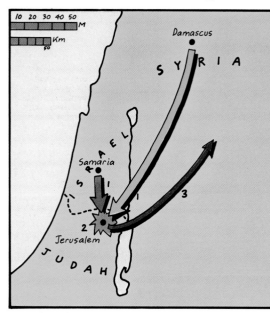

1  Israel and Syria (capitals: Samaria and Damascus) want Judah to join them in alliance against Assyria. Judah refuses. When Ahaz becomes king of Judah, Pekah of Israel and Rezin of Syria besiege Jerusalem together.

2  The people of Judah hear that Rezin's troops are in Israel and are terrified. But the prophet Isaiah ben Amoz advises Ahaz to stand firm. The siege will fail and Jerusalem be saved.

3  Ahaz refuses to listen and sends a message for help to Tiglath Pileser, Emperor of Assyria. The messenger takes gifts of silver and gold from the temple.

4  Rezin and Pekah fail to take Jerusalem.

5  The Assyrians arrive. They capture Damascus, kill Rezin and take his people into exile.

6  Ahaz goes to pay homage to Tiglath Pileser in Damascus. But in calling the Assyrians, Ahaz has lost Judah's political and religious independence. He returns to Jerusalem with new plans for the temple, where Assyrian gods will now be worshipped.

# Assyria Flexes Its Muscles

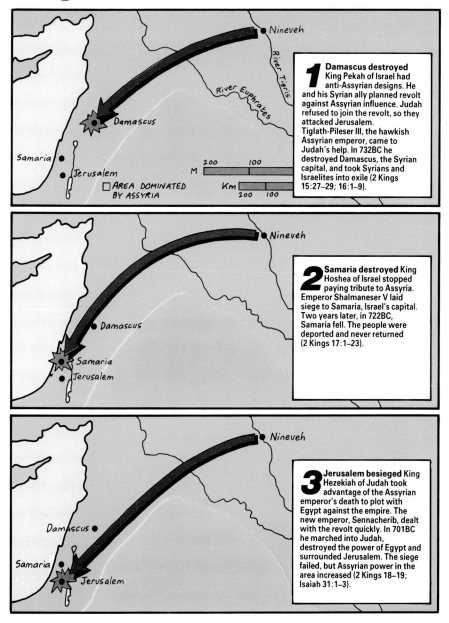

**1 Damascus destroyed**
King Pekah of Israel had anti-Assyrian designs. He and his Syrian ally planned revolt against Assyrian influence. Judah refused to join the revolt, so they attacked Jerusalem. Tiglath-Pileser III, the hawkish Assyrian emperor, came to Judah's help. In 732BC he destroyed Damascus, the Syrian capital, and took Syrians and Israelites into exile (2 Kings 15:27–29; 16:1–9).

**2 Samaria destroyed** King Hoshea of Israel stopped paying tribute to Assyria. Emperor Shalmaneser V laid siege to Samaria, Israel's capital. Two years later, in 722BC, Samaria fell. The people were deported and never returned (2 Kings 17:1–23).

**3 Jerusalem besieged** King Hezekiah of Judah took advantage of the Assyrian emperor's death to plot with Egypt against the empire. The new emperor, Sennacherib, dealt with the revolt quickly. In 701BC he marched into Judah, destroyed the power of Egypt and surrounded Jerusalem. The siege failed, but Assyrian power in the area increased (2 Kings 18–19; Isaiah 31:1–3).

# Israel Dragged into Exile

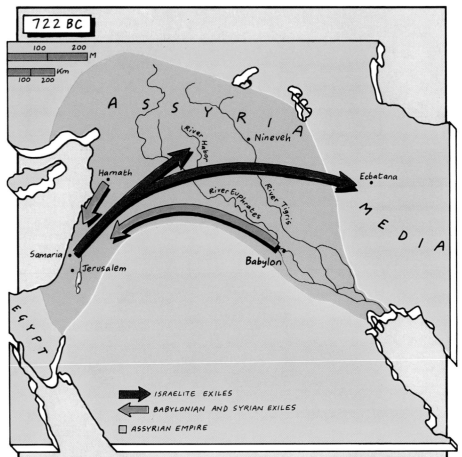

The prophets Amos and Hosea had predicted that Israel would be destroyed. The people had betrayed their faith, worshipping false gods and oppressing the poor of the land. They did not trust God, but instead relied on foreign alliances.

Hosea had warned: 'Israel flits about like a silly pigeon; first her people call on Egypt for help, and then they run to Assyria! But I will spread out a net and catch them like birds. . .'

The net fell in 722BC. Assyrian records claim that 27,290 Israelites were taken into captivity. They were deported to the region of the river Habor and to Media. For those who were taken to Media, this meant a journey of over 800 miles on foot.

Israel became a province of the Assyrian empire. The land was filled with foreign exiles forcibly removed from Babylon and Syria.

# The Prophets Speak

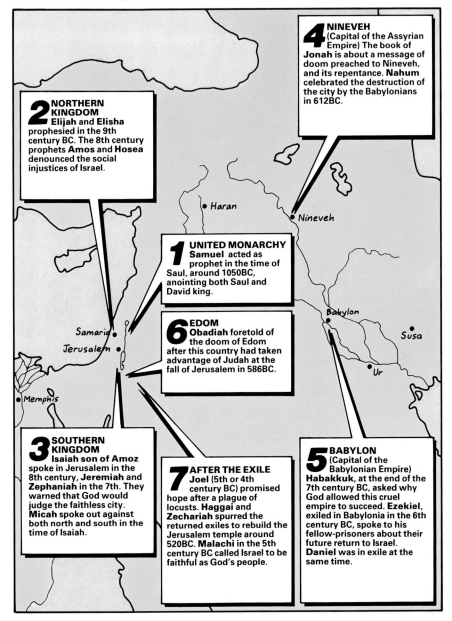

**4 NINEVEH**
(Capital of the Assyrian Empire) The book of **Jonah** is about a message of doom preached to Nineveh, and its repentance. **Nahum** celebrated the destruction of the city by the Babylonians in 612BC.

**2 NORTHERN KINGDOM**
**Elijah** and **Elisha** prophesied in the 9th century BC. The 8th century prophets **Amos** and **Hosea** denounced the social injustices of Israel.

• Haran

• Nineveh

**1 UNITED MONARCHY**
**Samuel** acted as prophet in the time of Saul, around 1050BC, anointing both Saul and David king.

Babylon•

**6 EDOM**
**Obadiah** foretold of the doom of Edom after this country had taken advantage of Judah at the fall of Jerusalem in 586BC.

Samaria •

Susa

Jerusalem •

• Ur

• Memphis

**3 SOUTHERN KINGDOM**
**Isaiah** son of Amoz spoke in Jerusalem in the 8th century, **Jeremiah** and **Zephaniah** in the 7th. They warned that God would judge the faithless city. **Micah** spoke out against both north and south in the time of Isaiah.

**7 AFTER THE EXILE**
**Joel** (5th or 4th century BC) promised hope after a plague of locusts. **Haggai** and **Zechariah** spurred the returned exiles to rebuild the Jerusalem temple around 520BC. **Malachi** in the 5th century BC called Israel to be faithful as God's people.

**5 BABYLON**
(Capital of the Babylonian Empire) **Habakkuk**, at the end of the 7th century BC, asked why God allowed this cruel empire to succeed. **Ezekiel**, exiled in Babylonia in the 6th century BC, spoke to his fellow-prisoners about their future return to Israel. **Daniel** was in exile at the same time.

# 6

# STARTING AGAIN

With Israel gone, Judah stood alone as the people of God. But the kings of Judah failed to learn from Israel's experience at the hands of the Assyrians. They flirted with foreign alliances against the superpower. And Judah, like Israel, was no longer faithful to God's Law. Prophets such as Isaiah son of Amoz and Jeremiah warned that the rottenness of society could only lead to disaster.

In a series of invasions, Jerusalem was captured, destroyed, and the leading citizens led into Babylonian exile. It seemed that all hope had been extinguished, that God had abandoned his people. But fifty years after the last people were taken into exile, the first group of returned exiles reached Jerusalem. The Persian Empire had replaced Babylon, opening its gates to allow captive peoples home.

# Starting Again

**Maps appearing in this chapter are:**

● **Like a Caged Bird** (page 73). King Hezekiah foolishly makes a bid for independence from Assyria. His allies are quickly defeated and he is besieged in Jerusalem by the emperor Sennacherib in 701 BC.

● **Josiah Purges the Gods** (page 74). In an attempt to reverse Judah's decline, King Josiah purifies his people's faith from false gods.

● **Josiah's Gamble** (page 75). Josiah's untimely death in battle against King Necho of Egypt in 609 BC.

● **Inside the Siege** (page 76). The prophet Jeremiah gives a vivid, insider's account of Nebuchadnezzar's siege of Jerusalem in 587 BC.

● **Jerusalem Falls** (page 77). Finally, after eighteen months, Jerusalem is finished. Judah follows Israel into Babylonian exile.

● **Kidnapped to Egypt** (page 78). Jeremiah is allowed by the Babylonians to stay free in Judah. But he is kidnapped by a gang of fugitives and taken to Egypt.

● **Who's Who in the Exile** (page 79). The dangerous years of Judah's exile called for outstanding courage and faith from the leaders of God's people.

● **Coming Home** (page 80). As promised in the book of Isaiah and by the prophet Ezekiel, the exile comes to an end. Four separate groups of people return to their homeland.

● **Rebuild My Temple!** (page 81). The Jerusalem temple is rebuilt on the ruins of Solomon's temple.

● **Swords and Trowels** (page 82). What did the different groups of returned exiles achieve in resettling in Judah?

**❝The Lord says, 'Assyria! I use Assyria like a club to punish those with whom I am angry.'❞**
Isaiah son of Amoz

**❝The Lord says,
'I will restore my people to their land and have mercy on every family;
Jerusalem will be rebuilt,
and its palace restored.
The people who live there will sing praise;
they will shout for joy.'❞**
Jeremiah prophesies the return from exile

**❝By the rivers of Babylon we sat down;
there we wept when we remembered Zion.❞**
An unknown exile (Psalm 137)

**❝When the Lord brought us back to Jerusalem,
it was like a dream!
How we laughed, how we sang for joy!❞**
Psalm 126

**❝My people, why should you be living in well-built houses while my Temple lies in ruins?❞**
Haggai, speaking to the returned exiles on God's behalf

# Like a Caged Bird

Hezekiah is besieged in Jerusalem by Sennacherib the Assyrian emperor.

**1** Sennacherib enters Palestine to crush a rebellion led by Egypt and Judah.

**2** He marches south, taking coastal towns, and defeats the Egyptians at Eltekeh.

**3** Simultaneously, the Assyrian commander besieges Jerusalem (according to Assyrian records), stopping Hezekiah's troops from defending the country. Sennacherib boasts in his own record of events: 'He himself (Hezekiah) I shut up like a caged bird within Jerusalem, his royal city.'

**4** Sennacherib lays siege to Lachish and after a long struggle reduces the fortified city to ashes.

**5** During the Lachish siege, Hezekiah sends gold and silver to the emperor, hoping to cool his anger. But Sennacherib's reply is to intensify the siege at Jerusalem. An Assyrian officer intimidates the people of the city. He says their God is powerless and resistance is useless. But the prophet Isaiah ben Amoz tells Hezekiah to stand firm and to trust God.

**6** Sennacherib attacks Libnah.

**7** The Jerusalem siege is suddenly withdrawn. Sennacherib returns to Assyria. He records that he took with him 200,150 people from the 46 captured towns of Judah.

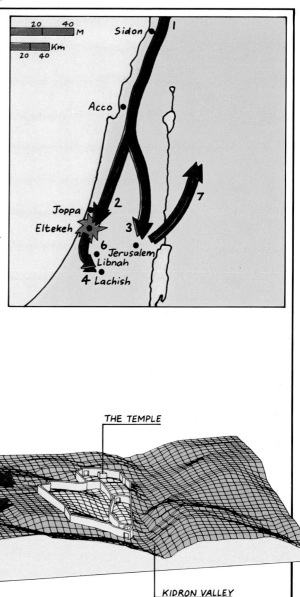

THE TEMPLE

KIDRON VALLEY

# Josiah Purges the Gods

Josiah was one of the few of Judah's kings who pleased God. During his reign, the Book of the Law (probably Deuteronomy) was discovered during repairs to the temple. Josiah was shocked by this forgotten book's condemnation of idol-worship. He began a purge.

**1** Took objects out of the temple used in worship of Baal and Asherah. Burnt them in the Kidron Valley.

**2** Destroyed the living quarters of the prostitutes in the temple.

**3** Tore down the altars of goat demons by one of the city gates.

**4** Desecrated altar of Molech in Hinnom Valley where children had been sacrificed.

**5** Removed horses and burnt chariots from the temple courtyard used in sun worship.

**6** Destroyed altars put up by various kings in the temple and in the palace.

**7** Destroyed Solomon's altars to Astarte, Chemosh and Molech south of the Mt of Olives.

Josiah also removed from office the priests of false gods and had many put to death. He also destroyed pagan altars in Bethel, and throughout Judah and Israel.

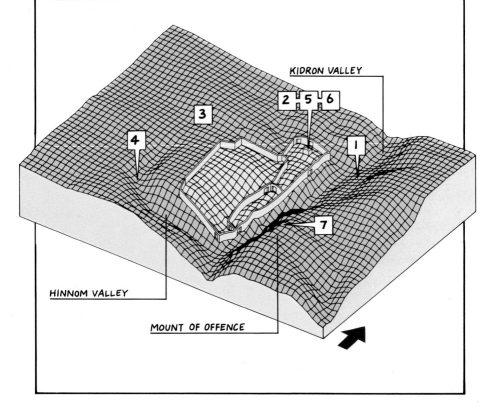

# Josiah's Gamble

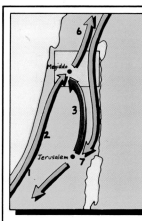

**1** The Assyrians are almost finished, while the Babylonian empire gains strength. Necho of Egypt marches north to help the Assyrians defeat Babylon. It is 609BC.

**2** Necho tells King Josiah of Judah not to attempt to stop him. Judah can remain neutral.

**3** Josiah refuses to listen. He marches to the plain of Megiddo and waits for Necho's army.

**4** Josiah could have attacked Necho on the coastal plain, or in the dangerous mountains and passes that lead out into the plain of Megiddo. It seems that he refused these easier battle sites to make an example of his enemy.

**5** Josiah disguises himself and goes into battle in his chariot. But he is wounded by Egyptian arrows and later dies. The battle is lost.

**6** Necho continues north. But the delay in his march means that the Assyrians are defeated in battle at the Syrian city of Carchemish. It is the end of the Assyrians as a power.

**7** Necho returns to Egypt, deposing Josiah's son, King Jehoahaz on the way. Judah is forced to pay a large tribute, and Necho installs Jehoiakim as his pocket ruler of the region.

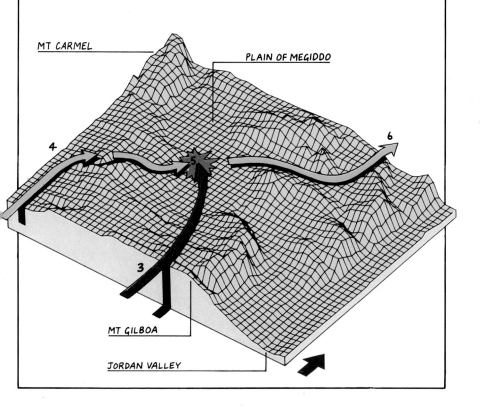

MT CARMEL

PLAIN OF MEGIDDO

MT GILBOA

JORDAN VALLEY

# Inside the Siege

Jerusalem had surrendered to Nebuchadnezzar, emperor of Babylon, in 597BC. He put Zedekiah on the throne. But Zedekiah hoped to throw off Babylonian rule. He became a focus for discontent in the region.

**1** Foreign ambassadors come to Zedekiah to plot against Babylon. Jeremiah the prophet wears a wooden yoke and urges them to submit to Babylon or be destroyed (Jeremiah 27).

**2** A false prophet, Hananiah, breaks Jeremiah's yoke in the temple. He says Babylon's power will be broken. Jeremiah starts to wear an iron yoke (Jeremiah 28).

**3** Nebuchadnezzar hears of Zedekiah's rebellion. He besieges Jerusalem with siege mounds (1 Kings 25:1–2).

**4** An Egyptian army approaches to relieve Jerusalem. The siege is lifted temporarily (Jeremiah 37:1–11).

**5** Jeremiah tries to leave the city on family business, but is arrested at the city gate (Jeremiah 37:12–21). Siege is renewed and food supplies run out.

**6** Jeremiah imprisoned in the palace courtyard. Thrown into a dry cistern for telling people to surrender to Babylon. Rescued later (Jeremiah 38:1–13).

**7** Kept in the courtyard, Jeremiah buys a field. He is confident that God will one day restore the land to Israel (Jeremiah 32:1–15).

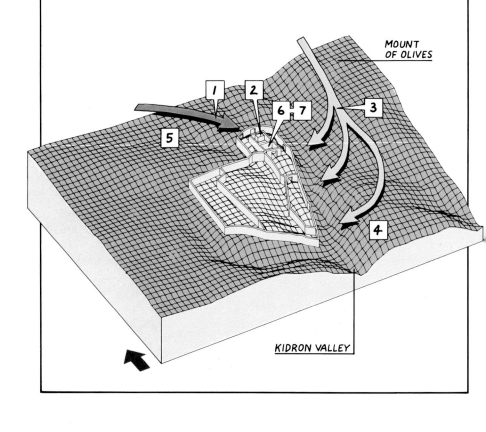

MOUNT OF OLIVES

KIDRON VALLEY

# Jerusalem Falls

**1** After 18 months of siege, in 586BC, the Babylonians break through Jerusalem's wall. Babylonian high officials enter the city and sit in the Middle Gate (Jeremiah 39:1–3).
**2** That night Zedekiah and his troops flee the city. They are soon captured near the Jordan Valley. Zedekiah's troops desert him, his sons are killed and he is blinded and led into exile (2 Kings 25:3–7).
**3** The commander of Babylon's army enters Jerusalem. He burns down the temple, palace and important buildings of the city. The walls are demolished.

**4** The people of Jerusalem are taken into exile, leaving only the poorest farm workers.
**5** The commander also removes the remaining temple equipment and anything of value (2 Kings 25:8–17).
**6** Jeremiah is spotted among the prisoners by the commander, who has orders from Nebuchadnezzar to release him. Jeremiah goes to live with his friend Gedaliah, new Babylonian governor of Judah (Jeremiah 40:1–6).

The rebellious city receives the punishment the prophets had predicted for it. The destruction is God's judgement on his unfaithful people.

# Kidnapped to Egypt

Jeremiah the prophet is forcibly taken to Egypt.

**1** Gedaliah is made governor of Judah by Nebuchadnezzar after the exile of King Zedekiah.

**2** Scattered exiles from Ammon, Moab and Edom return to Judah and help to gather the first harvest after the invasion.

**3** Ishmael, a member of the old royal family, leads a group of 10 escaped Judean soldiers to Mizpah. There they murder Gedaliah who they see as a puppet of Babylon.

**4** A large group, terrified of reprisals from Babylon, sets out for Egypt. At Bethlehem they kidnap Jeremiah, forcing him to go with them.

**5** The group travels as far as Tahpanhes in Egypt. They settle in various parts of the country.

**6** Eighteen years later, as Jeremiah prophesied, Nebuchadnezzar conquers Egypt and takes Jews from there into exile. Jeremiah himself probably died in Egypt.

2 Kings 25:22–26
Jeremiah 40–44

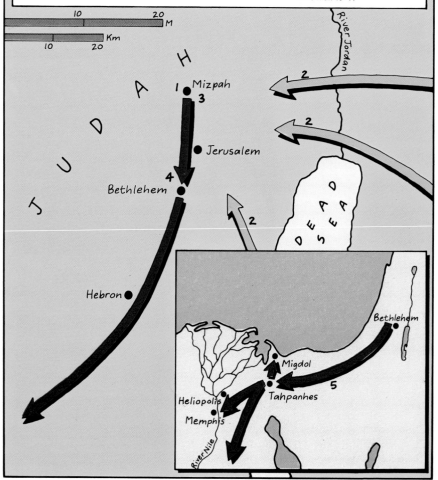

# Who's Who in the Exile

**Jehoiachin**
Exiled from Jerusalem at 18, having ruled 3 months. Probably kept under house arrest until 37 years later given a place of honour in the royal court. Seen as important figure by the Jewish exiles. Probably died during the exile. (2 Kings 24:1–15; 25:27–30.)

**Daniel**
Exiled with King Jehoiachin. Selected for training to serve in the royal court of Babylon. Daniel rose to become head of the royal advisers. Later in the exile, he was put in charge of all the Empire's governors. Some traditions say he returned to Jerusalem at the end of exile.

**Ezekiel**
Exiled with King Jehoiachin. He prophesied the destruction of Jerusalem, and later, that the exiles would return to Jerusalem with its rebuilt temple. Probably died before the end of exile.

**Esther and Mordecai**
Exiled with King Jehoiachin. Esther became queen to Xerxes, the Persian emperor, not long before the return of Nehemiah to Jerusalem. With her cousin Mordecai, she prevented the persecution of Jews throughout the Persian Empire. Mordecai became a powerful figure in Xerxes' court.

Nineveh

Babylon

Nippur

Susa

Jerusalem

Memphis

**Jeremiah**
Forced to go to Egypt at the start of Judah's exile by a group who fled after killing the Babylonian governor of Judah. He spent the rest of his life in Egypt. (Jeremiah 43.)

**Ezra**
A high official in the Persian Empire – 'minister for Jewish affairs'. Emperor Artaxerxes I sent him to Jerusalem to reform the people there in accordance with Jewish Law. He led the fourth group of exiles home. (Ezra 7.)

**Nehemiah**
Cupbearer to Artaxerxes I, Nehemiah was sent by the emperor in 445BC to rebuild the walls of Jerusalem. He led the third group of exiles home. (Nehemiah 1 – 2).

**Ordinary people**
Many Jews in the exile became prosperous (see Ezra 2:68–69). Living in ghettos in Babylon and other places, they stayed together. But despite their wealth they despaired at the loss of their land and heritage. Psalm 137 expresses their feelings.

☐ MENTIONED IN EARLY PART OF EXILE
☐ MENTIONED DURING EXILE
■ MENTIONED AT END OF EXILE

# Coming Home

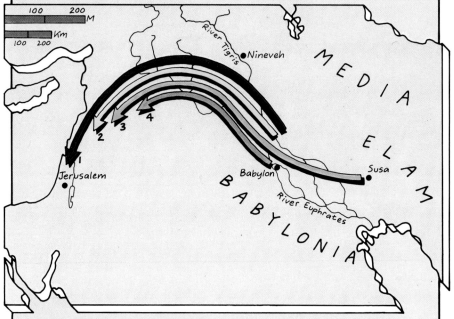

In 539BC the Babylonian Empire was taken over by Cyrus, the Persian king. He issued commands that all the displaced exiles should return home to worship their own gods. The exiles were free to return to Judah.

**1 Sheshbazzar,** a Jewish exile, is made governor of Judah, 537BC. He is given the temple treasures taken by Nebuchadnezzar, and returns to Judah with a group of exiles (Ezra 1).

**2 Zerubbabel** (grandson of King Jehoiachin) **and Joshua,** a priest, lead another group home in 525BC.

**3 Nehemiah,** cupbearer in the Persian court to King Artaxerxes I, is sent to Jerusalem in 445BC to repair Jerusalem's walls. An armed guard escorts him (Nehemiah 1–2).

**4 Ezra,** a scholar and Jewish priest, is given royal authority to renew the religious practices of Jerusalem. He leads exiles home in 428BC (Ezra 7:1–10).

**Inset**

**1** Priests, Levites and others settle in or near Jerusalem.

**2** Musicians, temple guards, workmen settle locally.

**3** Rest of returned exiles settle in the towns of their ancestors.

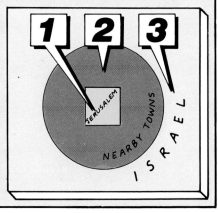

# Rebuild My Temple!

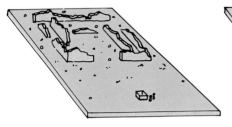

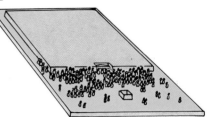

**1** *Ezra 3:1–6* On the site of Solomon's temple, 50 years after its destruction, returned exiles rebuild the altar and begin to worship God there daily again.

**2** *Ezra 3:7–13* The site is cleared and foundations for the new temple laid. The people sing and shout for joy. Some people present had seen the previous temple.

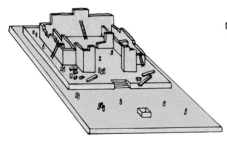

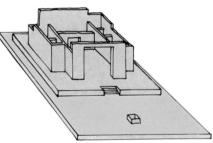

**3** *Ezra 4:1–5* The work continues, but the local inhabitants try to stop the returned exiles from continuing.

**4** *Ezra 4:24* The work on the temple stops for 16 years. This is partly due to opposition, but also because of laziness (Haggai 1:2–8).

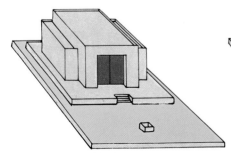

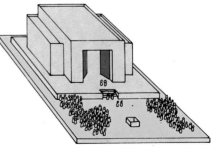

**5** *Ezra 5:1–6:15* Under the encouragement of the prophets Haggai and Zechariah, the building continues again. The governor of the region complains, but Emperor Darius orders the temple to be built. It is finally completed after another 4 years.

**6** *Ezra 6:16–22* The temple is joyfully dedicated, and it starts to be used regularly for worship. This temple stood for nearly 500 years – longer than its predecessor (Solomon's) or its successor (Herod's).

# Swords and Trowels

What did the different groups of
returning exiles achieve in
Jerusalem?

**1** Rebuilding the temple.
The first 2 groups under
Sheshbazzar and
Zerubbabel began to rebuild the
destroyed temple. This was
financed partly by the Persian
treasury and partly by the people
themselves. Despite opposition
from those who had not been
exiled, the temple was completed
about 22 years later (Ezra 3–6).

**2** Reconstructing the
walls. Nehemiah's return
to Jerusalem signalled the
start of work on Jerusalem's
walls. This was about 70 years
after the temple had been
completed. Again there was local
opposition. The builders were
determined to complete the
work, even when it came to
holding a trowel with one hand
and a sword with the other
(Nehemiah 1:1–7:7).

**3** Renewing the faith. Ezra
was commanded by the
Persian Emperor to make
sure that the Jewish Law was
being observed fully in Jerusalem
and Judah. The covenant was
renewed at a public reading of the
Law 'in the square just inside the
Water Gate' (Nehemiah 8:1). Ezra
also dealt with the problem of
mixed marriages (Ezra 7–10,
Nehemiah 8–9).

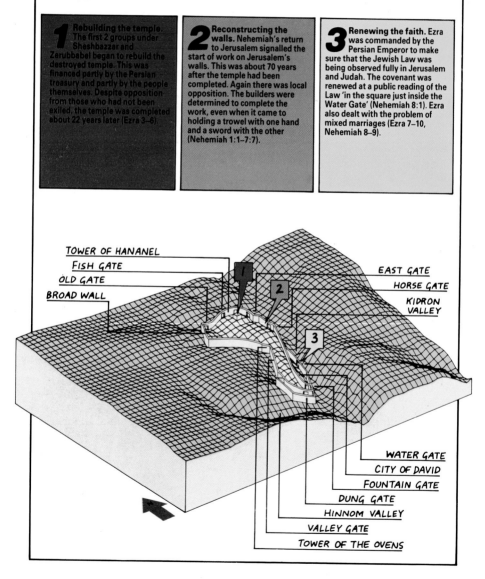

TOWER OF HANANEL
FISH GATE
OLD GATE
BROAD WALL

EAST GATE
HORSE GATE
KIDRON VALLEY

WATER GATE
CITY OF DAVID
FOUNTAIN GATE
DUNG GATE
HINNOM VALLEY
VALLEY GATE
TOWER OF THE OVENS

# 7

# JESUS SEEN AND HEARD

Four centuries after the last voice of the Old Testament, the Jewish people were once again under the rule of a powerful empire. Judea was a pocket-sized province of the Roman world kept under tight control by taxation and troops of occupation. Many Jews longed for liberation from their oppression, hoping for a 'Messiah' (or deliverer) in the mould of King David.

John the Baptist and Jesus started their work, but neither fitted the popular role of the warrior-Messiah. Within three years, John had been beheaded and Jesus was handed over to the Roman authorities to be crucified. But Jesus was raised from death. He was the expected Messiah in a far greater sense than anyone had imagined.

# Jesus Seen and Heard

**Maps appearing in this chapter are:**

● **The Birth of Jesus** (page 85). Jesus is born around 7 BC. His parents have to take him to Egypt as a child because of the murderous jealousy of Herod the Great.

● **John the Baptizer** (page 86). John begins his work, calling people to repent and baptizing them in the River Jordan.

● **On Herod's Birthday** (page 87). John is arrested and put to death by Herod Antipas around AD 29.

● **Jesus Starts his Work** (page 88). Jesus the Nazareth carpenter is baptized by John and calls his first disciples.

● **A Journey North** (page 89). Events from early in Jesus' ministry in Samaria and Galilee.

● **Asleep in the Storm** (page 90). Jesus' work was characterized by acts of healing, miracles over the forces of nature and casting out demons.

● **Among the Gentiles** (page 91). Jesus concentrated mainly on Jewish people, but on several occasions he worked among non-Jews.

● **Who Do You Say I Am?** (page 92). Jesus tests public opinion about himself –

and then asks his disciples to decide who he is.

● **Capernaum and Bethany** (page 93). Although Jesus and his followers spent long periods on the road, he found a home in the north and south.

● **Lazarus, Come Out!** (page 94). Jesus raises Lazarus back to life, and his action provokes a hostile reaction from his enemies. They plot to kill him.

● **Jesus Enters Jerusalem** (page 95). Jesus goes to Jerusalem for the last time, knowing that he will be betrayed. He is given a hero's welcome and drives thieving merchants out of the temple.

● **The Last 24 Hours** (page 96). AD 33. Jesus has a last meal with his disciples, is betrayed, arrested, tried and put to death by the Romans.

● **We Are Witnesses** (page 97). The first Christians' belief in Jesus' resurrection was backed up by a large number of people who said they had seen him alive.

● **Followers of Jesus** (page 98). During his ministry, Jesus was followed by a great variety of men and women.

**66 'The Spirit of the Lord is on me, because he has anointed me to preach good news to the poor. He has sent me to proclaim freedom for the prisoners and recovery of sight for the blind, to release the oppressed, to proclaim the year of the Lord's favour.' Today this scripture is fulfilled in your hearing. 99**
Jesus, at the beginning of his ministry

**66 I baptize you with water for repentance. But after me will come one who is more powerful than I, whose sandals I am not fit to carry. He will baptize you with the Holy Spirit and with fire. 99**
John the Baptist

**66 You are the Christ, the Son of the living God. 99**
Peter's confession of Jesus

# The Birth of Jesus

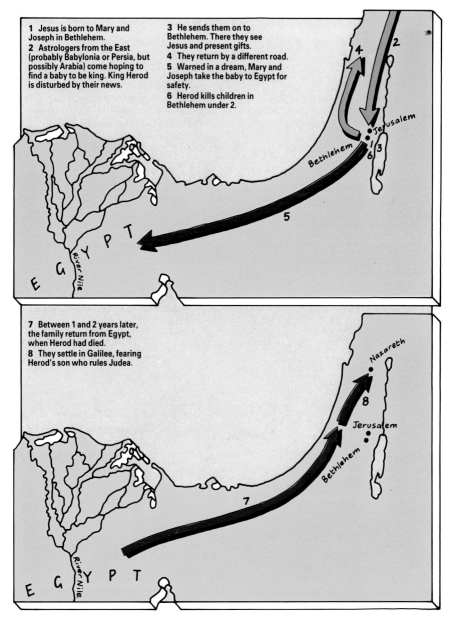

1  Jesus is born to Mary and Joseph in Bethlehem.
2  Astrologers from the East (probably Babylonia or Persia, but possibly Arabia) come hoping to find a baby to be king. King Herod is disturbed by their news.

3  He sends them on to Bethlehem. There they see Jesus and present gifts.
4  They return by a different road.
5  Warned in a dream, Mary and Joseph take the baby to Egypt for safety.
6  Herod kills children in Bethlehem under 2.

7  Between 1 and 2 years later, the family return from Egypt, when Herod had died.
8  They settle in Galilee, fearing Herod's son who rules Judea.

# John the Baptizer

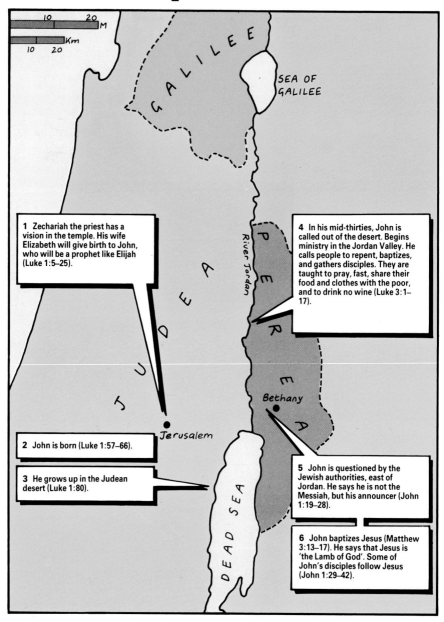

**1**  Zechariah the priest has a vision in the temple. His wife Elizabeth will give birth to John, who will be a prophet like Elijah (Luke 1:5–25).

**4**  In his mid-thirties, John is called out of the desert. Begins ministry in the Jordan Valley. He calls people to repent, baptizes, and gathers disciples. They are taught to pray, fast, share their food and clothes with the poor, and to drink no wine (Luke 3:1–17).

**2**  John is born (Luke 1:57–66).

**3**  He grows up in the Judean desert (Luke 1:80).

**5**  John is questioned by the Jewish authorities, east of Jordan. He says he is not the Messiah, but his announcer (John 1:19–28).

**6**  John baptizes Jesus (Matthew 3:13–17). He says that Jesus is 'the Lamb of God'. Some of John's disciples follow Jesus (John 1:29–42).

SEA OF GALILEE

GALILEE

JUDEA

PEREA

River Jordan

Bethany

Jerusalem

DEAD SEA

# On Herod's Birthday

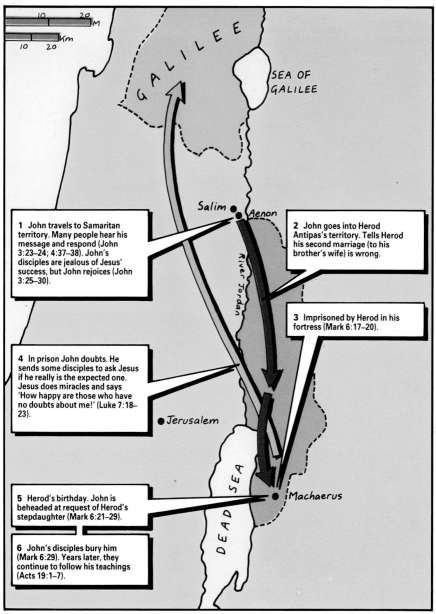

1 John travels to Samaritan territory. Many people hear his message and respond (John 3:23–24; 4:37–38). John's disciples are jealous of Jesus' success, but John rejoices (John 3:25–30).

2 John goes into Herod Antipas's territory. Tells Herod his second marriage (to his brother's wife) is wrong.

3 Imprisoned by Herod in his fortress (Mark 6:17–20).

4 In prison John doubts. He sends some disciples to ask Jesus if he really is the expected one. Jesus does miracles and says 'How happy are those who have no doubts about me!' (Luke 7:18–23).

5 Herod's birthday. John is beheaded at request of Herod's stepdaughter (Mark 6:21–29).

6 John's disciples bury him (Mark 6:29). Years later, they continue to follow his teachings (Acts 19:1–7).

# Jesus Starts his Work

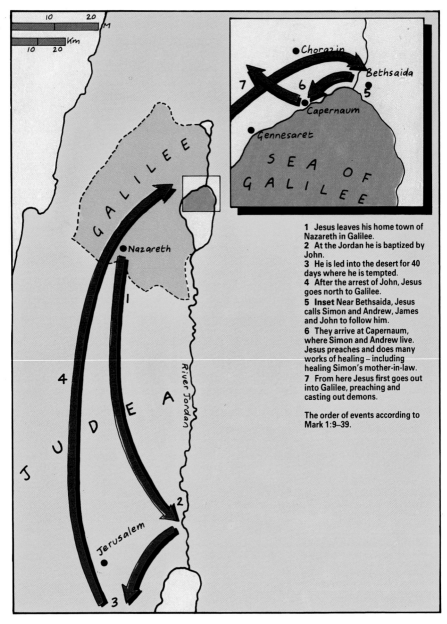

1  Jesus leaves his home town of Nazareth in Galilee.

2  At the Jordan he is baptized by John.

3  He is led into the desert for 40 days where he is tempted.

4  After the arrest of John, Jesus goes north to Galilee.

5  **Inset** Near Bethsaida, Jesus calls Simon and Andrew, James and John to follow him.

6  They arrive at Capernaum, where Simon and Andrew live. Jesus preaches and does many works of healing – including healing Simon's mother-in-law.

7  From here Jesus first goes out into Galilee, preaching and casting out demons.

The order of events according to Mark 1:9–39.

# A Journey North

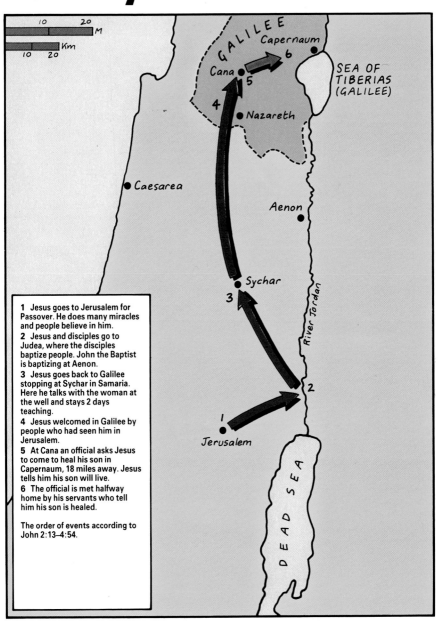

1 Jesus goes to Jerusalem for Passover. He does many miracles and people believe in him.

2 Jesus and disciples go to Judea, where the disciples baptize people. John the Baptist is baptizing at Aenon.

3 Jesus goes back to Galilee stopping at Sychar in Samaria. Here he talks with the woman at the well and stays 2 days teaching.

4 Jesus welcomed in Galilee by people who had seen him in Jerusalem.

5 At Cana an official asks Jesus to come to heal his son in Capernaum, 18 miles away. Jesus tells him his son will live.

6 The official is met halfway home by his servants who tell him his son is healed.

The order of events according to John 2:13–4:54.

# Asleep in the Storm

**1** Jesus calls his 12 disciples on a hill.
**2** Jesus and the disciples 'went home' (to Capernaum, where Jesus made his headquarters). Jesus was so busy teaching the crowds that he hardly had time to eat.
**3** The disciples and Jesus set out on the Sea of Galilee in the evening.
**4** A great storm threatens to sink the boat – but Jesus is asleep. The disciples wake him and he calms the storm with a command.

**5** They arrive in the territory of Gerasa or Gadara. There Jesus casts out from a man a mob of demons into some pigs.
**6** Jesus and the disciples re-cross the lake. Jesus brings Jairus's daughter to life and heals a woman who touched his coat.
**7** They go to Nazareth, where Jesus is rejected. He sends out his 12 disciples to preach, heal and cast out demons.

The order of events according to Mark 3:13–6:13. Many incidental details show these to be eye-witness accounts, probably told to Mark by Peter.

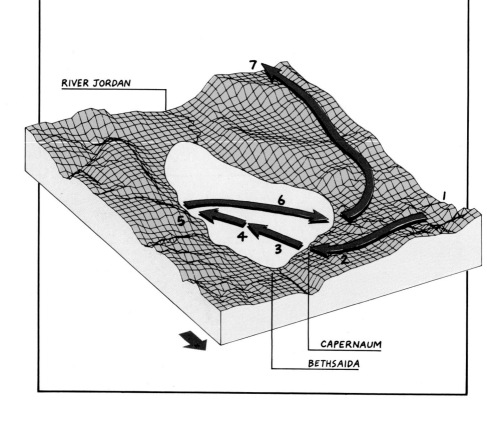

RIVER JORDAN

CAPERNAUM

BETHSAIDA

# Among the Gentiles

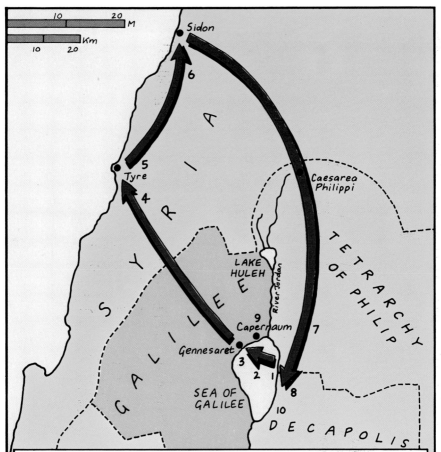

1 After the feeding of 5,000 Jesus sends the disciples in a boat to Bethsaida.

2 A headwind slows their progress. At dead of night Jesus walks on the water to them.

3 Driven off course, they reach Gennesaret. They stay some time, Jesus healing many sick people in the region.

4 Jesus goes to territory near Tyre – possibly alone. He tries to keep his visit secret.

5 A Gentile woman begs him to drive a demon out of her daughter. Jesus refuses, but she persists. He delivers the girl at a distance.

6 He travels north near Sidon.

7 He goes down to the region of Decapolis ('Ten Towns'). There is no mention that he preaches or enters any towns.

8 Here he heals a deaf man with a speech impediment. His miracle-making reputation spreads. (Reconstruction of events in Mark 6:45–56; 7:24–37.)

On two other separate occasions Jesus responded to the needs of non-Jews:

9 Heals the servant of a Roman officer who has implicit faith in him (Luke 7:1–10).

10 Drives out a host of demons from a man in Decapolis (Mark 5:1–20).

# Who Do You Say I Am?

**1** Jesus and his disciples are at Bethsaida, where he heals a blind man.

**2** They travel to the area around Caesarea Philippi. Jesus asks the disciples who people think he is. Peter says he believes Jesus to be the Messiah. Jesus tells them about his coming death.

**3** Six days later Jesus takes Peter, James and John up a high mountain (probably Mt Hermon) where he is transfigured. At the foot of the mountain he drives an evil spirit out of a boy.

**4** Jesus and the disciples travel on through Galilee. Jesus talks about his coming death.

**5** At Capernaum Jesus confronts his disciples about their rival claims to be the greatest disciple.

The order of events according to Mark 8:22–9:37.

Mt Hermon
▲ **3**

Caesarea Philippi

**2**

**4**

LAKE HULEH

River Jordan

G A L I L E E

**5**
Capernaum

**I**
Bethsaida

SEA OF GALILEE

5    10
M
5    10
Km

# Capernaum and Bethany

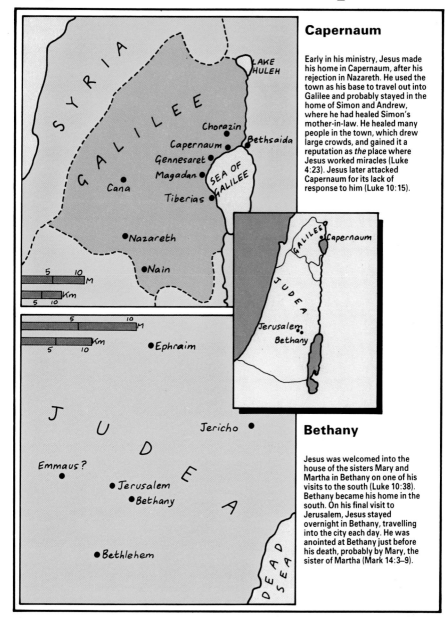

## Capernaum

Early in his ministry, Jesus made his home in Capernaum, after his rejection in Nazareth. He used the town as his base to travel out into Galilee and probably stayed in the home of Simon and Andrew, where he had healed Simon's mother-in-law. He healed many people in the town, which drew large crowds, and gained it a reputation as *the* place where Jesus worked miracles (Luke 4:23). Jesus later attacked Capernaum for its lack of response to him (Luke 10:15).

## Bethany

Jesus was welcomed into the house of the sisters Mary and Martha in Bethany on one of his visits to the south (Luke 10:38). Bethany became his home in the south. On his final visit to Jerusalem, Jesus stayed overnight in Bethany, travelling into the city each day. He was anointed at Bethany just before his death, probably by Mary, the sister of Martha (Mark 14:3–9).

# Lazarus, Come Out!

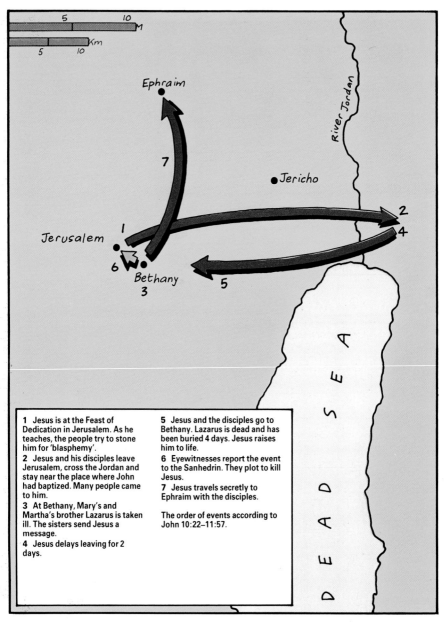

1  Jesus is at the Feast of Dedication in Jerusalem. As he teaches, the people try to stone him for 'blasphemy'.

2  Jesus and his disciples leave Jerusalem, cross the Jordan and stay near the place where John had baptized. Many people came to him.

3  At Bethany, Mary's and Martha's brother Lazarus is taken ill. The sisters send Jesus a message.

4  Jesus delays leaving for 2 days.

5  Jesus and the disciples go to Bethany. Lazarus is dead and has been buried 4 days. Jesus raises him to life.

6  Eyewitnesses report the event to the Sanhedrin. They plot to kill Jesus.

7  Jesus travels secretly to Ephraim with the disciples.

The order of events according to John 10:22–11:57.

# Jesus Enters Jerusalem

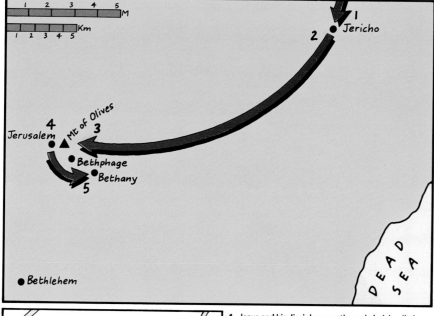

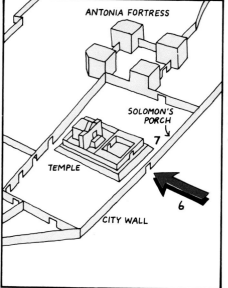

1 Jesus and his disciples pass through Jericho. (Luke records the meeting with Zacchaeus here.)

2 On the way out of Jericho, followed by a large crowd, Jesus heals blind Bartimaeus.

3 On the Mt of Olives, Jesus sends 2 of his disciples to collect a donkey, as arranged, from its owner in either Bethphage or Bethany.

4 Jesus rides the donkey into Jerusalem, and a crowd welcomes him as the Messiah.

5 They spend the night in Bethany.

6 Next morning, they re-enter Jerusalem.

7 In the temple, in Solomon's Porch, Jesus throws out the dishonest merchants.

The order of events according to Mark 10:46–11:19.

# The Last 24 Hours

**1** Jesus and disciples eat the Passover at a secret location – the upper room (Mark 14:12–26).
**2** Judas leaves at night to betray Jesus (John 13:21–30).
**3** In Gethsemane, Jesus prays while disciples sleep (Mark 14:32–42).
**4** Judas leads Roman soldiers and temple guards to arrest Jesus. Disciples flee (Mark 14:43–52).
**5** Jesus before Annas (father-in-law to Caiaphas), to decide the charge (John 18:12–14).

**6** Jesus before Caiaphas (High Priest) and the Jewish Council. Witnesses disagree, Jesus refuses to answer questions. Convicted of blasphemy. Peter denies knowing Jesus (Mark 14:53–72).
**7** Early morning, taken to Pilate's palace, charged with political crimes. Pilate thinks he is innocent (Luke 23:1–5).
**8** Pilate sends Jesus to Herod Antipas (who had executed John the Baptist) at his palace. Jesus refuses to talk, Herod and soldiers dress him up as king (Luke 23:6–12).

**9** Pilate offers to release Jesus, crowd chooses Barabbas. Jesus condemned on Gabbatha, pavement outside palace (John 18:38–19:16).
**10** Judas hears and tries to return his betrayal payment to the priests.
**11** Judas commits suicide (Matthew 27:3–10).
**12** Soldiers mock Jesus (Matthew 27:27–31).
**13** On Golgotha, 'the Skull', Jesus is crucified (Luke 27:32–44).

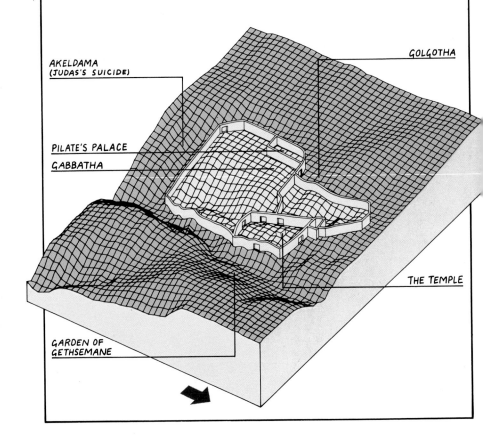

AKELDAMA
(JUDAS'S SUICIDE)

GOLGOTHA

PILATE'S PALACE

GABBATHA

THE TEMPLE

GARDEN OF
GETHSEMANE

# We Are Witnesses

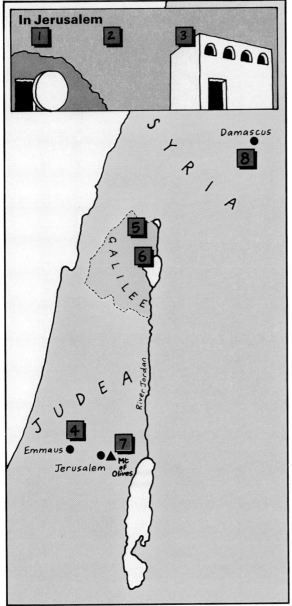

1 **At the tomb** Mary Magdalene meets Jesus (John 20:11–18, Mark 16:9–11).

2 **Near the tomb** Mary Magdalene and 'the other Mary' (Matthew 28:9–10).

3 **In the upper room** As the disciples were eating (Mark 16:14–18). Jesus allows them to feel him and he eats fish (Luke 24:36–49). Behind locked doors without Thomas (John 20:19–23). With Thomas (John 20:24–29).

4 **On the Emmaus road** Cleopas and another disciple (Luke 24:13–35, Mark 16:12–13).

5 **On 'the hill in Galilee'** Eleven disciples (Matthew 28:16–20).

6 **By Lake Tiberias** (the Sea of Galilee). Peter, Thomas, Nathanael, James, John and 2 others are cooked breakfast by Jesus (John 21:1–22).

7 **On the Mt of Olives** ('as far as Bethany'). Jesus ascends to heaven (Luke 24:50–51, Acts 1:6–11).

8 **On the Damascus road** Jesus appears to Saul (Acts 9:1–9).

Paul in 1 Corinthians 15:5–7 records separate appearances to Peter, James (brother of Jesus), and 'to more than 500 of his followers at once'.

Acts 1:3 notes that Jesus appeared many times over a 40 day period after his resurrection.

# Followers of Jesus

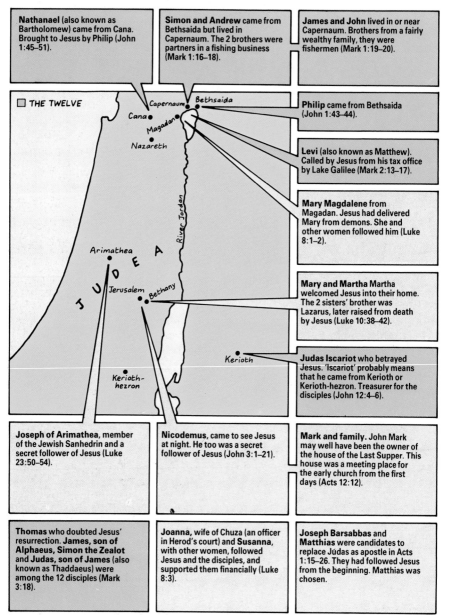

**Nathanael** (also known as Bartholomew) came from Cana. Brought to Jesus by Philip (John 1:45–51).

**Simon and Andrew** came from Bethsaida but lived in Capernaum. The 2 brothers were partners in a fishing business (Mark 1:16–18).

**James and John** lived in or near Capernaum. Brothers from a fairly wealthy family, they were fishermen (Mark 1:19–20).

THE TWELVE

Capernaum  Bethsaida

Cana

Magadan

Nazareth

River Jordan

Arimathea

J U D E A

Jerusalem  Bethany

Kerioth

Kerioth-hezron

**Philip** came from Bethsaida (John 1:43–44).

**Levi** (also known as Matthew). Called by Jesus from his tax office by Lake Galilee (Mark 2:13–17).

**Mary Magdalene** from Magadan. Jesus had delivered Mary from demons. She and other women followed him (Luke 8:1–2).

**Mary and Martha** Martha welcomed Jesus into their home. The 2 sisters' brother was Lazarus, later raised from death by Jesus (Luke 10:38–42).

**Judas Iscariot** who betrayed Jesus. 'Iscariot' probably means that he came from Kerioth or Kerioth-hezron. Treasurer for the disciples (John 12:4–6).

**Joseph of Arimathea**, member of the Jewish Sanhedrin and a secret follower of Jesus (Luke 23:50–54).

**Nicodemus**, came to see Jesus at night. He too was a secret follower of Jesus (John 3:1–21).

**Mark and family.** John Mark may well have been the owner of the house of the Last Supper. This house was a meeting place for the early church from the first days (Acts 12:12).

**Thomas** who doubted Jesus' resurrection. **James, son of Alphaeus, Simon the Zealot** and **Judas, son of James** (also known as Thaddaeus) were among the 12 disciples (Mark 3:18).

**Joanna**, wife of Chuza (an officer in Herod's court) and **Susanna**, with other women, followed Jesus and the disciples, and supported them financially (Luke 8:3).

**Joseph Barsabbas** and **Matthias** were candidates to replace Judas as apostle in Acts 1:15–26. They had followed Jesus from the beginning. Matthias was chosen.

# 8

# FOLLOWERS OF THE WAY

Seven weeks after the resurrection of Jesus, the church was born. It was the Day of Pentecost; Jerusalem was full of Jewish pilgrims. The Holy Spirit fell on the followers of Jesus with dramatic results: three thousand pilgrims believed and were baptized. The church remained in Jerusalem until Stephen was stoned to death for preaching. The persecution which followed meant that Christians were scattered, taking the good news with them.

Peter was responsible for the conversion of a non-Jewish centurion, Cornelius, and those who believed that the gospel was only for Jews criticized him for this. But Peter defended his actions, and the doors were opened wide for anyone – regardless of race – to become Christians. What had started as just another small Jewish sect was quickly becoming an international movement.

# Followers of the Way

**Maps appearing in this chapter are:**

**❝All the people of Israel, then, are to
know for sure that this Jesus, whom
you crucified, is the one that God has
made Lord and Messiah.❞**
Peter preaches on the Day of
Pentecost

**❝We gave you strict orders not to
teach in the name of this man, but see
what you have done! You have spread
your teaching all over Jerusalem, and
you want to make us responsible for
his death!❞**
Caiaphas, the High Priest, accuses the
apostles

**❝Look! I see heaven open and the
Son of Man standing at the right hand
of God.❞**
Stephen, at his martyrdom

**❝My dear friends, do not be
surprised at the painful test you are
suffering, as though something
unusual were happening to you. Rather
be glad that you are sharing Christ's
sufferings, so that you may be full of
joy when his glory is revealed.❞**
Peter, writing to the churches he
founded

# The Jerusalem Believers

**1** Disciples see Jesus for the last time before his ascension on Mt of Olives.

**2** About 10 days later, Jerusalem is full of pilgrims for the Feast of Pentecost. In the upper room, all the believers are filled with the Holy Spirit. A crowd gathers, Peter preaches, 3,000 are converted.

**3** The believers share possessions, work miracles, meet together daily in the temple.

**4** At the 'Beautiful Gate' in the temple, Peter and John heal a lame man. As they preach to a crowd, they are arrested.

**5** The Jewish Council warn them not to talk about Jesus.

**6** The believers meet regularly in Solomon's Porch in the temple. Large numbers are added to the group.

**7** All the apostles are arrested and jailed. But at night they are miraculously released. At dawn they preach in the temple.

**8** They are taken to the Jewish Council, flogged and forbidden to preach.

**9** The group chooses 7 men to manage the funds. One of them, Stephen, is arrested and stoned to death outside the city. This triggers off violent persecution and the believers scatter with the good news.

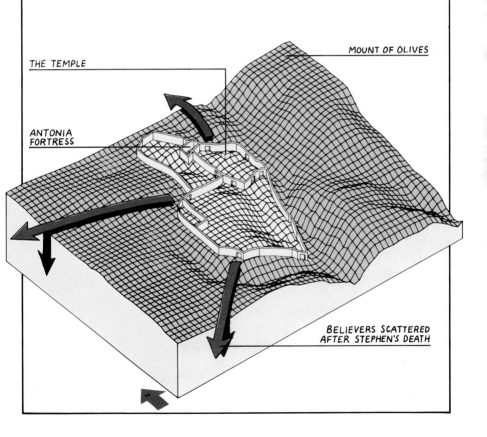

MOUNT OF OLIVES

THE TEMPLE

ANTONIA FORTRESS

BELIEVERS SCATTERED AFTER STEPHEN'S DEATH

# The Message Explodes

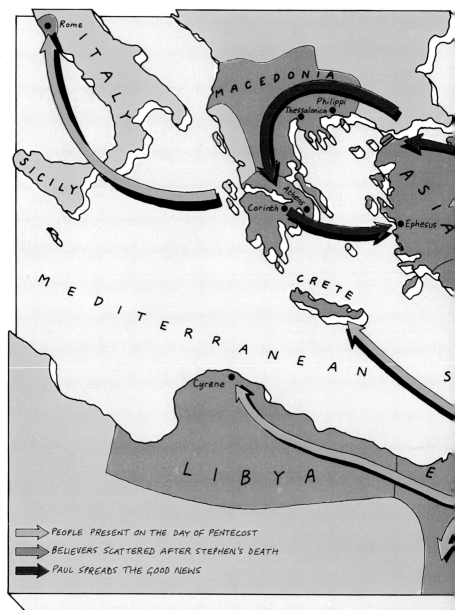

PEOPLE PRESENT ON THE DAY OF PENTECOST
BELIEVERS SCATTERED AFTER STEPHEN'S DEATH
PAUL SPREADS THE GOOD NEWS

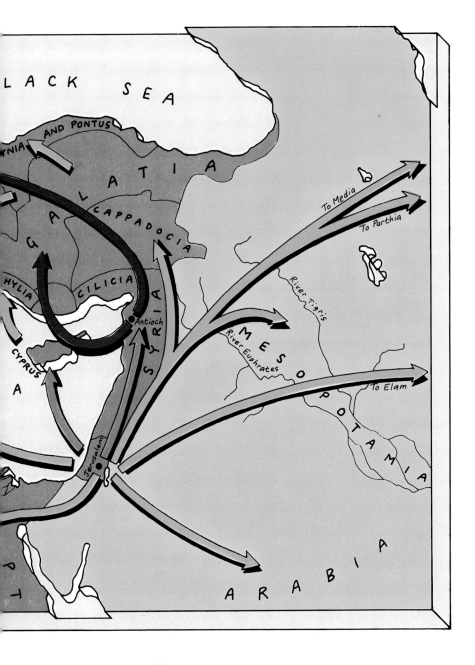

# Philip's Exploits

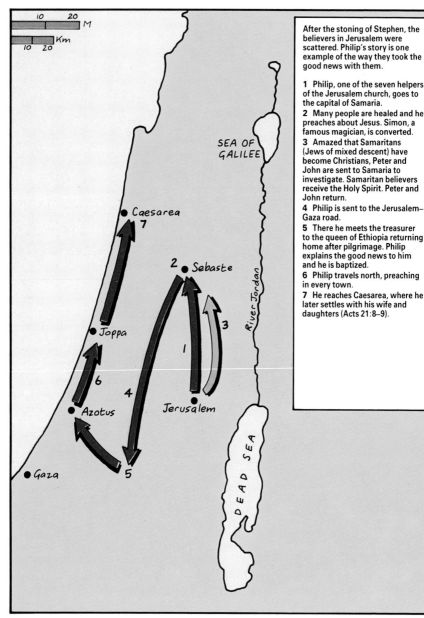

After the stoning of Stephen, the believers in Jerusalem were scattered. Philip's story is one example of the way they took the good news with them.

**1** Philip, one of the seven helpers of the Jerusalem church, goes to the capital of Samaria.

**2** Many people are healed and he preaches about Jesus. Simon, a famous magician, is converted.

**3** Amazed that Samaritans (Jews of mixed descent) have become Christians, Peter and John are sent to Samaria to investigate. Samaritan believers receive the Holy Spirit. Peter and John return.

**4** Philip is sent to the Jerusalem–Gaza road.

**5** There he meets the treasurer to the queen of Ethiopia returning home after pilgrimage. Philip explains the good news to him and he is baptized.

**6** Philip travels north, preaching in every town.

**7** He reaches Caesarea, where he later settles with his wife and daughters (Acts 21:8–9).

# Antioch: Gentile Church

Antioch was the third largest city of the Roman Empire. It was non-Jewish, made up of many different races. It soon became the centre of Gentile Christianity.

**1** Stephen is martyred and the believers are scattered everywhere (Acts 8:1–4).

**2** Some travel as far as Antioch. They tell the message to Jews only (Acts 11:19).

**3** Other believers come from Cyprus and north Africa. They preach to Gentiles in Antioch with dramatic results (Acts 11:20–21).

**4** The Jerusalem church sends Barnabas, a trusted leader, to investigate.

**5** He is pleased at the church's progress. He collects Saul from Tarsus and the two stay to teach (Acts 11:22–26).

**6** Here, the name 'Christians' is coined.

**7 Inset** The Antioch church soon becomes strong. The believers send relief money to the mother church in Jerusalem (Acts 11:27–30).

**8** Paul and Barnabas are sent out by the church in Antioch. They are the first messengers of the gospel to foreign countries (Acts 13:1–3).

The leaders in Antioch give a cross-section of this cosmopolitan church (Acts 13:1):
**Barnabas**, a Jew from Cyprus.
**Simeon** (called the Black) probably from Africa.
**Lucius** from Cyrene, a north African city.
**Manaen**, foster-brother to Herod Antipas.
**Saul**, a Jew from Roman Tarsus, later to become Paul the apostle.

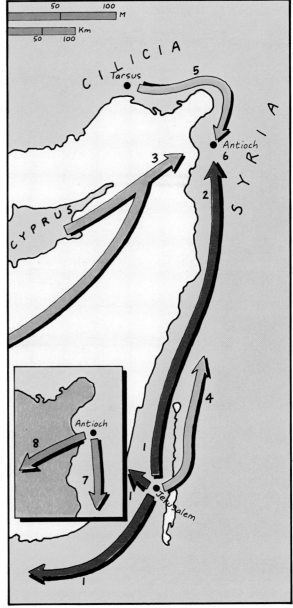

# Travelling the Roman World

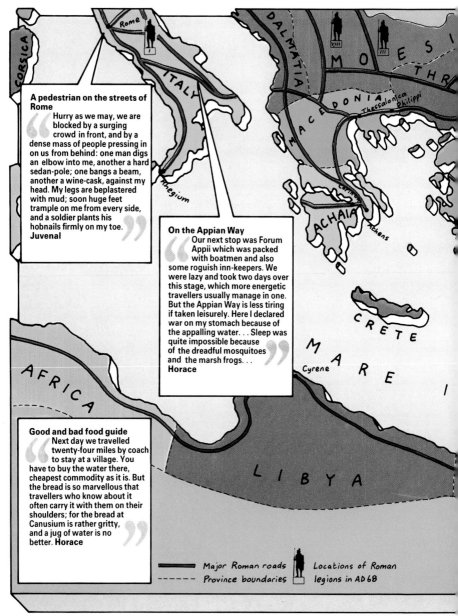

**A pedestrian on the streets of Rome**

Hurry as we may, we are blocked by a surging crowd in front, and by a dense mass of people pressing in on us from behind: one man digs an elbow into me, another a hard sedan-pole; one bangs a beam, another a wine-cask, against my head. My legs are beplastered with mud; soon huge feet trample on me from every side, and a soldier plants his hobnails firmly on my toe. **Juvenal**

**On the Appian Way**

Our next stop was Forum Appii which was packed with boatmen and also some roguish inn-keepers. We were lazy and took two days over this stage, which more energetic travellers usually manage in one. But the Appian Way is less tiring if taken leisurely. Here I declared war on my stomach because of the appalling water. . . Sleep was quite impossible because of the dreadful mosquitoes and the marsh frogs. . . **Horace**

**Good and bad food guide**

Next day we travelled twenty-four miles by coach to stay at a village. You have to buy the water there, cheapest commodity as it is. But the bread is so marvellous that travellers who know about it often carry it with them on their shoulders; for the bread at Canusium is rather gritty, and a jug of water is no better. **Horace**

———— Major Roman roads
‒‒‒‒‒‒ Province boundaries

Locations of Roman legions in AD 68

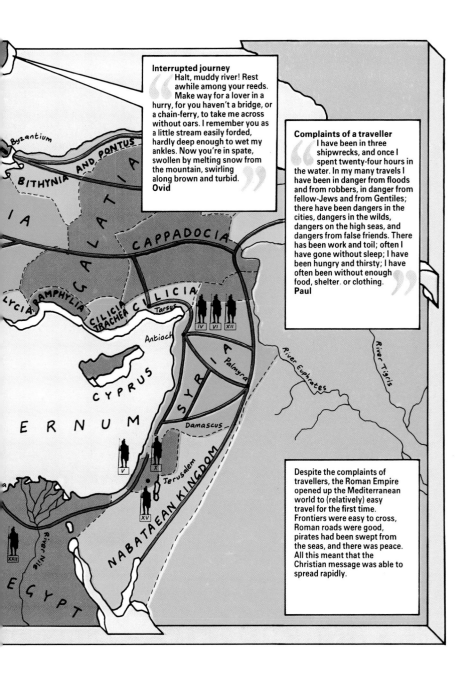

**Interrupted journey**
Halt, muddy river! Rest awhile among your reeds. Make way for a lover in a hurry, for you haven't a bridge, or a chain-ferry, to take me across without oars. I remember you as a little stream easily forded, hardly deep enough to wet my ankles. Now you're in spate, swollen by melting snow from the mountain, swirling along brown and turbid.
**Ovid**

**Complaints of a traveller**
I have been in three shipwrecks, and once I spent twenty-four hours in the water. In my many travels I have been in danger from floods and from robbers, in danger from fellow-Jews and from Gentiles; there have been dangers in the cities, dangers in the wilds, dangers on the high seas, and dangers from false friends. There has been work and toil; often I have gone without sleep; I have been hungry and thirsty; I have often been without enough food, shelter, or clothing.
**Paul**

Despite the complaints of travellers, the Roman Empire opened up the Mediterranean world to (relatively) easy travel for the first time. Frontiers were easy to cross, Roman roads were good, pirates had been swept from the seas, and there was peace. All this meant that the Christian message was able to spread rapidly.

# Peter's Journeys

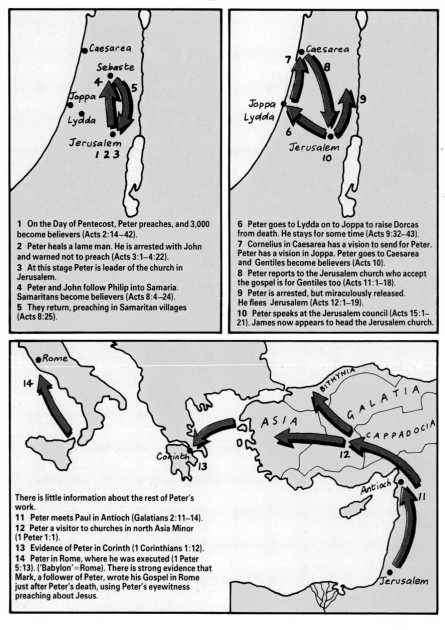

1  On the Day of Pentecost, Peter preaches, and 3,000 become believers (Acts 2:14–42).

2  Peter heals a lame man. He is arrested with John and warned not to preach (Acts 3:1–4:22).

3  At this stage Peter is leader of the church in Jerusalem.

4  Peter and John follow Philip into Samaria. Samaritans become believers (Acts 8:4–24).

5  They return, preaching in Samaritan villages (Acts 8:25).

6  Peter goes to Lydda on to Joppa to raise Dorcas from death. He stays for some time (Acts 9:32–43).

7  Cornelius in Caesarea has a vision to send for Peter. Peter has a vision in Joppa. Peter goes to Caesarea and Gentiles become believers (Acts 10).

8  Peter reports to the Jerusalem church who accept the gospel is for Gentiles too (Acts 11:1–18).

9  Peter is arrested, but miraculously released. He flees Jerusalem (Acts 12:1–19).

10  Peter speaks at the Jerusalem council (Acts 15:1–21). James now appears to head the Jerusalem church.

There is little information about the rest of Peter's work.

11  Peter meets Paul in Antioch (Galatians 2:11–14).

12  Peter a visitor to churches in north Asia Minor (1 Peter 1:1).

13  Evidence of Peter in Corinth (1 Corinthians 1:12).

14  Peter in Rome, where he was executed (1 Peter 5:13). ('Babylon'=Rome). There is strong evidence that Mark, a follower of Peter, wrote his Gospel in Rome just after Peter's death, using Peter's eyewitness preaching about Jesus.

# 9

# ON THE ROAD
# WITH PAUL

Saul (he came to be known as Paul after his conversion) was born in Tarsus as a Roman citizen. He became a strict Pharisee in Jerusalem and in the early days of the church's life was notorious in his crusade to stamp out belief in Jesus. His abrupt conversion made many Christians suspicious at first that this was another tactic in his persecutions.

But Paul had been transformed by his meeting with Jesus, risen and alive, on the Damascus road. He was to become the apostle to the Gentiles, taking the message of Jesus from the streets of Jerusalem to the imperial palace in Rome. For twenty years he travelled: preaching, starting Christian communities, encouraging and teaching. And during this time he also wrote the letters that became a major part of the New Testament.

# On the Road With Paul

Maps appearing in this chapter are:

❝The man who formerly persecuted
us is now preaching the faith he once
tried to destroy.❞

The report of Paul's conversion in the
early church

❝I am the least of all the apostles – I
do not even deserve to be called an
apostle, because I persecuted God's
church. But by God's grace I am what I
am, and the grace that he gave me was
not without effect.❞

Paul

❝I have fought the good fight, I have
finished the race, I have kept the faith.
Now there is in store for me the crown
of righteousness, which the Lord, the
righteous judge, will award to me on
that day – and not only to me, but also
to all who have longed for his
appearing.❞

Paul writes to Timothy just before his
death

# Midday Outside Damascus

Saul's early life until his conversion.

**1** Saul (later called Paul) is born and spends his early years in Tarsus – an important Roman city. He is born a Roman citizen (Acts 22:25–29).

**2** Taken to Jerusalem as a young boy and educated by the well-known teacher Gamaliel (Acts 22:3). He is a Pharisee.

**3** When Stephen is stoned to death for his faith, Saul holds the stoners' coats. He becomes a violent persecutor of the church, given authority to imprison Christians (Acts 26:9–11). He even travels to foreign cities to root them out.

**4** On one such visit, Saul travels to Damascus to arrest believers. At midday, near the city, he has a vision of Jesus. A voice says, 'Saul, Saul, why do you persecute me?'

**5** In the city a believer called Ananias visits Saul. His blindness is healed and he is baptized (Acts 9:1–19).

**6** Saul stays for 3 years in Damascus, preaching in the synagogues. At some point in Acts 9:19–22 he went into the desert of Arabia (Galatians 1:15–17), and returned to continue his work there.

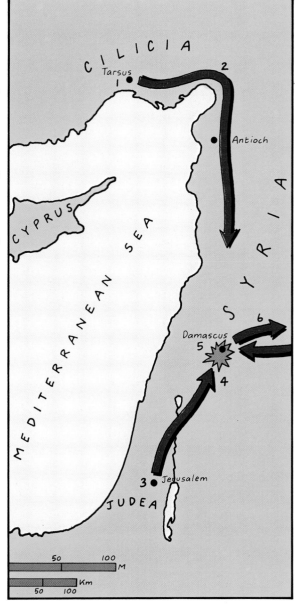

# Apostle to the Gentiles

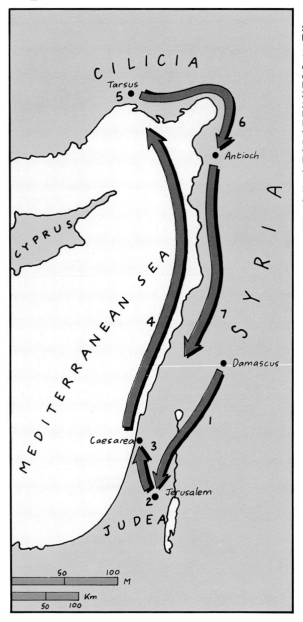

Saul's work after Damascus and before his first journey.

**1** Three years after his conversion, Saul is forced to escape from the Jews of Damascus in a basket (Acts 9:23–25).

**2** He goes to Jerusalem to see Peter. The believers still suspect him, but Barnabas introduces him to them. He talks with Peter and meets James. But after only 2 weeks he has to be smuggled out because of opposition from some Jews (Acts 9:26–30, Galatians 1:18–20).

**3** Saul is taken to Caesarea.

**4** From there he leaves for his home city of Tarsus (Acts 9:30).

**5** He spends 10 years in Tarsus. During this time he visits places in Cilicia and Syria. He is still unknown personally to believers in Judea (Galatians 1:21–24).

**6** Barnabas (who had been sent to work in the church in Antioch) goes to find Saul in Tarsus. He brings him back to Antioch. They teach together for 1 year (Acts 11:25–26).

**7** Saul, Barnabas and Titus go to Jerusalem with famine relief money for Judea. They meet privately with the church leaders. Despite some disagreements, the leaders recognize Saul's ministry to the Gentiles (Acts 11:27–30, Galatians 2:1–10).

# Mission to the Galatians

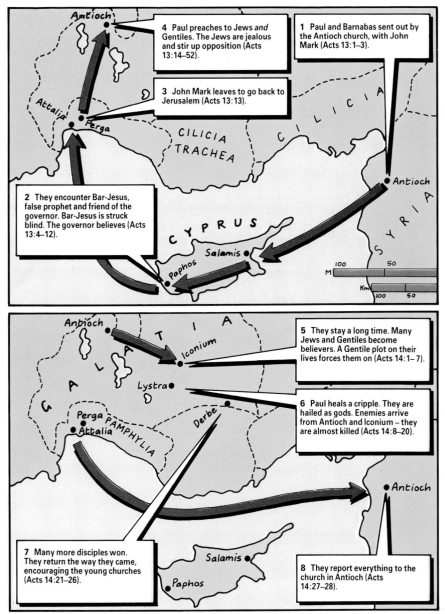

**4** Paul preaches to Jews *and* Gentiles. The Jews are jealous and stir up opposition (Acts 13:14–52).

**1** Paul and Barnabas sent out by the Antioch church, with John Mark (Acts 13:1–3).

**3** John Mark leaves to go back to Jerusalem (Acts 13:13).

**2** They encounter Bar-Jesus, false prophet and friend of the governor. Bar-Jesus is struck blind. The governor believes (Acts 13:4–12).

**5** They stay a long time. Many Jews and Gentiles become believers. A Gentile plot on their lives forces them on (Acts 14:1–7).

**6** Paul heals a cripple. They are hailed as gods. Enemies arrive from Antioch and Iconium – they are almost killed (Acts 14:8–20).

**7** Many more disciples won. They return the way they came, encouraging the young churches (Acts 14:21–26).

**8** They report everything to the church in Antioch (Acts 14:27–28).

# Mission to Greece

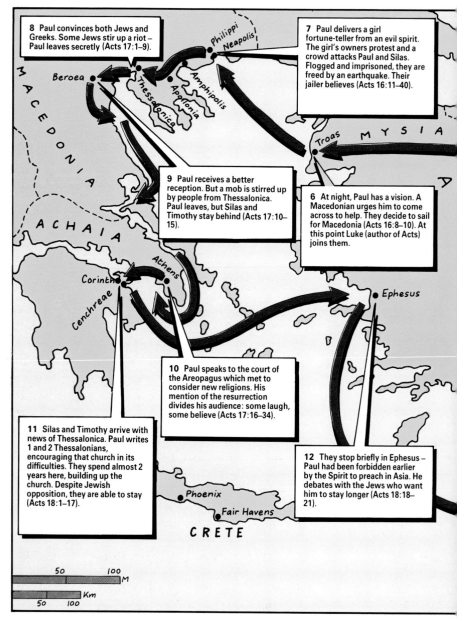

**8** Paul convinces both Jews and Greeks. Some Jews stir up a riot – Paul leaves secretly (Acts 17:1–9).

**7** Paul delivers a girl fortune-teller from an evil spirit. The girl's owners protest and a crowd attacks Paul and Silas. Flogged and imprisoned, they are freed by an earthquake. Their jailer believes (Acts 16:11–40).

**9** Paul receives a better reception. But a mob is stirred up by people from Thessalonica. Paul leaves, but Silas and Timothy stay behind (Acts 17:10–15).

**6** At night, Paul has a vision. A Macedonian urges him to come across to help. They decide to sail for Macedonia (Acts 16:8–10). At this point Luke (author of Acts) joins them.

**10** Paul speaks to the court of the Areopagus which met to consider new religions. His mention of the resurrection divides his audience: some laugh, some believe (Acts 17:16–34).

**11** Silas and Timothy arrive with news of Thessalonica. Paul writes 1 and 2 Thessalonians, encouraging that church in its difficulties. They spend almost 2 years here, building up the church. Despite Jewish opposition, they are able to stay (Acts 18:1–17).

**12** They stop briefly in Ephesus – Paul had been forbidden earlier by the Spirit to preach in Asia. He debates with the Jews who want him to stay longer (Acts 18:18–21).

Philippi
Neapolis
Beroea
Amphipolis
Thessalonica
Apollonia
MACEDONIA
Troas
MYSIA
ACHAIA
Corinth
Athens
Cenchreae
Ephesus
Phoenix
Fair Havens
CRETE

50      100
M
Km
50      100

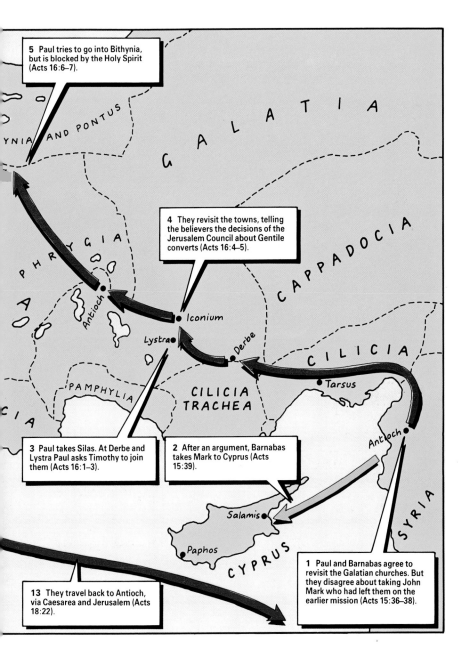

5  Paul tries to go into Bithynia, but is blocked by the Holy Spirit (Acts 16:6–7).

4  They revisit the towns, telling the believers the decisions of the Jerusalem Council about Gentile converts (Acts 16:4–5).

3  Paul takes Silas. At Derbe and Lystra Paul asks Timothy to join them (Acts 16:1–3).

2  After an argument, Barnabas takes Mark to Cyprus (Acts 15:39).

1  Paul and Barnabas agree to revisit the Galatian churches. But they disagree about taking John Mark who had left them on the earlier mission (Acts 15:36–38).

13  They travel back to Antioch, via Caesarea and Jerusalem (Acts 18:22).

GALATIA

YNIA    AND PONTUS

PHRYGIA

CAPPADOCIA

Antioch

Iconium

Lystra

Derbe

CILICIA

Tarsus

PAMPHYLIA

CILICIA TRACHEA

Antioch

SYRIA

Salamis

Paphos

CYPRUS

# The Corinthian Affair

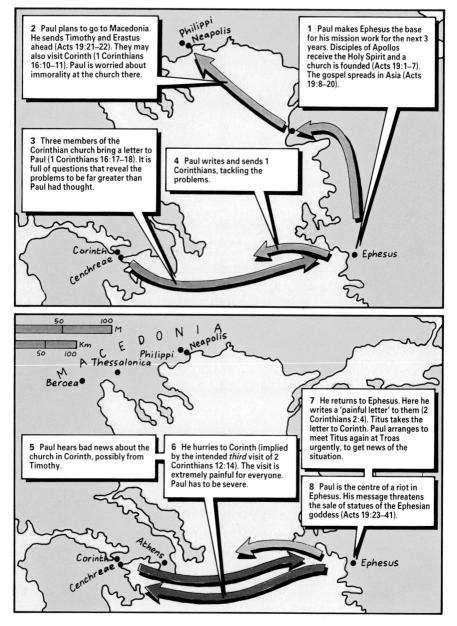

**2** Paul plans to go to Macedonia. He sends Timothy and Erastus ahead (Acts 19:21–22). They may also visit Corinth (1 Corinthians 16:10–11). Paul is worried about immorality at the church there.

**1** Paul makes Ephesus the base for his mission work for the next 3 years. Disciples of Apollos receive the Holy Spirit and a church is founded (Acts 19:1–7). The gospel spreads in Asia (Acts 19:8–20).

**3** Three members of the Corinthian church bring a letter to Paul (1 Corinthians 16:17–18). It is full of questions that reveal the problems to be far greater than Paul had thought.

**4** Paul writes and sends 1 Corinthians, tackling the problems.

**5** Paul hears bad news about the church in Corinth, possibly from Timothy.

**6** He hurries to Corinth (implied by the intended *third* visit of 2 Corinthians 12:14). The visit is extremely painful for everyone. Paul has to be severe.

**7** He returns to Ephesus. Here he writes a 'painful letter' to them (2 Corinthians 2:4). Titus takes the letter to Corinth. Paul arranges to meet Titus again at Troas urgently, to get news of the situation.

**8** Paul is the centre of a riot in Ephesus. His message threatens the sale of statues of the Ephesian goddess (Acts 19:23–41).

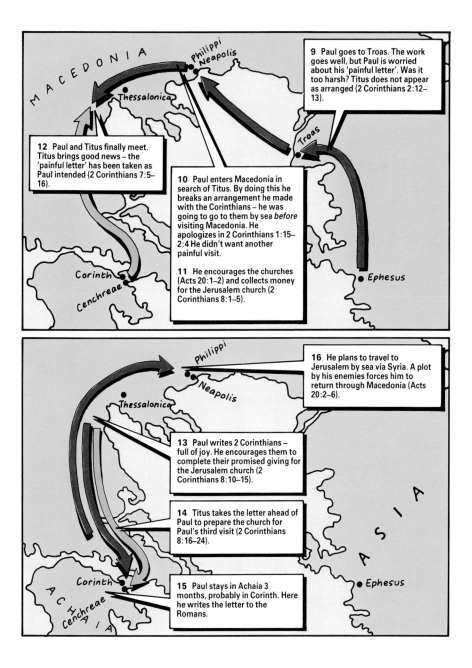

9  Paul goes to Troas. The work goes well, but Paul is worried about his 'painful letter'. Was it too harsh? Titus does not appear as arranged (2 Corinthians 2:12–13).

12  Paul and Titus finally meet. Titus brings good news – the 'painful letter' has been taken as Paul intended (2 Corinthians 7:5–16).

10  Paul enters Macedonia in search of Titus. By doing this he breaks an arrangement he made with the Corinthians – he was going to go to them by sea *before* visiting Macedonia. He apologizes in 2 Corinthians 1:15–2:4 He didn't want another painful visit.

11  He encourages the churches (Acts 20:1–2) and collects money for the Jerusalem church (2 Corinthians 8:1–5).

16  He plans to travel to Jerusalem by sea via Syria. A plot by his enemies forces him to return through Macedonia (Acts 20:2–6).

13  Paul writes 2 Corinthians – full of joy. He encourages them to complete their promised giving for the Jerusalem church (2 Corinthians 8:10–15).

14  Titus takes the letter ahead of Paul to prepare the church for Paul's third visit (2 Corinthians 8:16–24).

15  Paul stays in Achaia 3 months, probably in Corinth. Here he writes the letter to the Romans.

# To Jerusalem

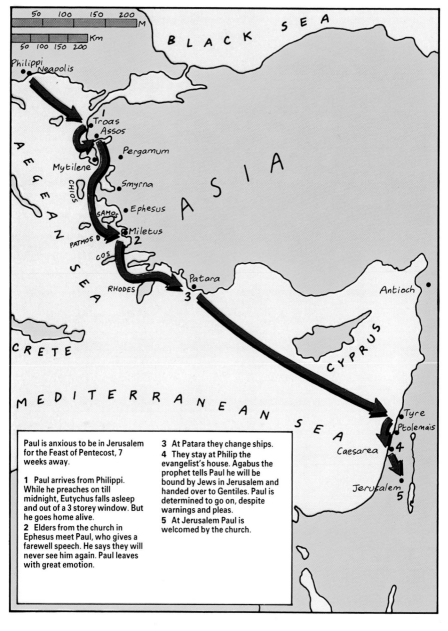

Paul is anxious to be in Jerusalem for the Feast of Pentecost, 7 weeks away.

**1** Paul arrives from Philippi. While he preaches on till midnight, Eutychus falls asleep and out of a 3 storey window. But he goes home alive.
**2** Elders from the church in Ephesus meet Paul, who gives a farewell speech. He says they will never see him again. Paul leaves with great emotion.

**3** At Patara they change ships.
**4** They stay at Philip the evangelist's house. Agabus the prophet tells Paul he will be bound by Jews in Jerusalem and handed over to Gentiles. Paul is determined to go on, despite warnings and pleas.
**5** At Jerusalem Paul is welcomed by the church.

# I Appeal to Caesar!

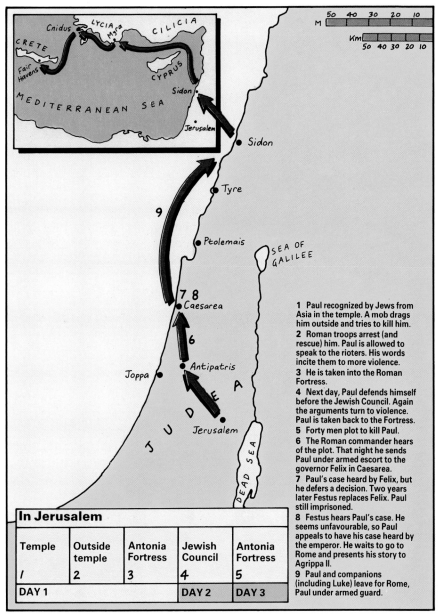

1  Paul recognized by Jews from Asia in the temple. A mob drags him outside and tries to kill him.

2  Roman troops arrest (and rescue) him. Paul is allowed to speak to the rioters. His words incite them to more violence.

3  He is taken into the Roman Fortress.

4  Next day, Paul defends himself before the Jewish Council. Again the arguments turn to violence. Paul is taken back to the Fortress.

5  Forty men plot to kill Paul.

6  The Roman commander hears of the plot. That night he sends Paul under armed escort to the governor Felix in Caesarea.

7  Paul's case heard by Felix, but he defers a decision. Two years later Festus replaces Felix. Paul still imprisoned.

8  Festus hears Paul's case. He seems unfavourable, so Paul appeals to have his case heard by the emperor. He waits to go to Rome and presents his story to Agrippa II.

9  Paul and companions (including Luke) leave for Rome, Paul under armed guard.

## In Jerusalem

| Temple | Outside temple | Antonia Fortress | Jewish Council | Antonia Fortress |
|--------|----------------|------------------|----------------|------------------|
| 1 | 2 | 3 | 4 | 5 |
| DAY 1 | | | DAY 2 | DAY 3 |

# Storm and Shipwreck

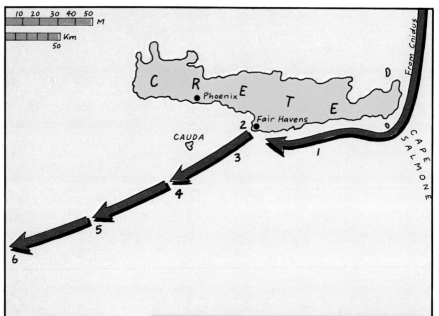

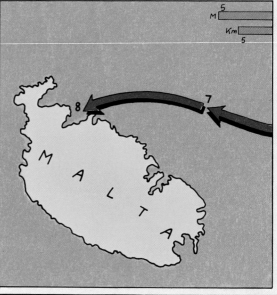

1 In bad weather Paul's ship reaches Fair Havens.

2 They shelter there until the end of September – the end of the safe sailing season. The captain decides to winter in the better harbour at Phoenix.

3 On route to Phoenix they are blown out to sea.

4 South of Cauda they pull the boat on board, lower the sail and let the ship run.

5 Next day they jettison ship's cargo.

6 Next day they jettison ship's equipment.

7 **Inset** Night 14 of the storm, land is near. Sailors try to escape but fail. After eating, they lighten the ship.

8 Ship hits a sandbank in a bay and begins to break up. All hands are saved.

# And So We Came to Rome

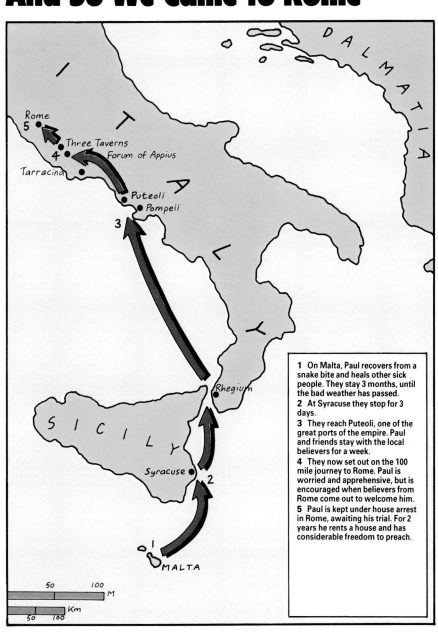

1 On Malta, Paul recovers from a snake bite and heals other sick people. They stay 3 months, until the bad weather has passed.

2 At Syracuse they stop for 3 days.

3 They reach Puteoli, one of the great ports of the empire. Paul and friends stay with the local believers for a week.

4 They now set out on the 100 mile journey to Rome. Paul is worried and apprehensive, but is encouraged when believers from Rome come out to welcome him.

5 Paul is kept under house arrest in Rome, awaiting his trial. For 2 years he rents a house and has considerable freedom to preach.

# Letters for New Churches

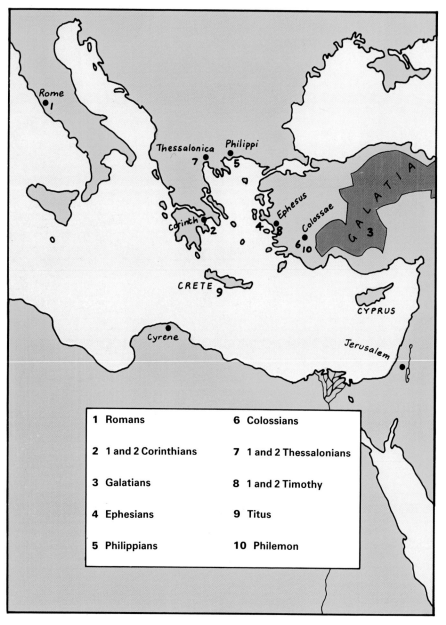

Rome
1

Thessalonica   Philippi
7               5

Corinth
2

Ephesus
4   8

Colossae
6  10

GALATIA
3

CRETE
9

Cyrene

CYPRUS

Jerusalem

| 1 | Romans | 6 | Colossians |
|---|--------|---|------------|
| 2 | 1 and 2 Corinthians | 7 | 1 and 2 Thessalonians |
| 3 | Galatians | 8 | 1 and 2 Timothy |
| 4 | Ephesians | 9 | Titus |
| 5 | Philippians | 10 | Philemon |

# Paul's Troubleshooter

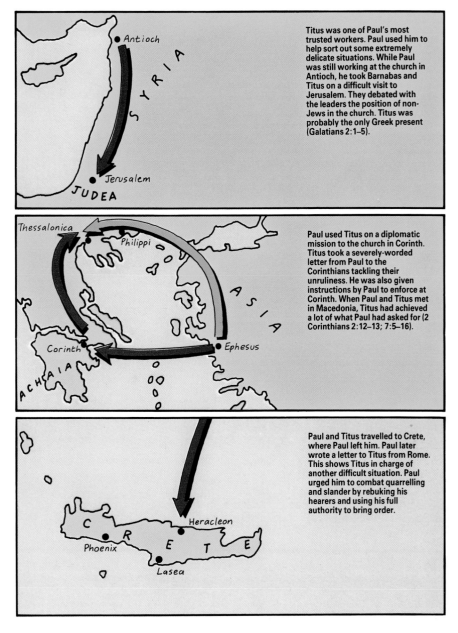

Titus was one of Paul's most trusted workers. Paul used him to help sort out some extremely delicate situations. While Paul was still working at the church in Antioch, he took Barnabas and Titus on a difficult visit to Jerusalem. They debated with the leaders the position of non-Jews in the church. Titus was probably the only Greek present (Galatians 2:1–5).

Paul used Titus on a diplomatic mission to the church in Corinth. Titus took a severely-worded letter from Paul to the Corinthians tackling their unruliness. He was also given instructions by Paul to enforce at Corinth. When Paul and Titus met in Macedonia, Titus had achieved a lot of what Paul had asked for (2 Corinthians 2:12–13; 7:5–16).

Paul and Titus travelled to Crete, where Paul left him. Paul later wrote a letter to Titus from Rome. This shows Titus in charge of another difficult situation. Paul urged him to combat quarrelling and slander by rebuking his hearers and using his full authority to bring order.

# Paul's Final Footprints

Three books of the New
Testament give a few brief
glimpses of Paul's activity beyond
the end of Acts. They were
written to two young church
leaders who had worked under
Paul.

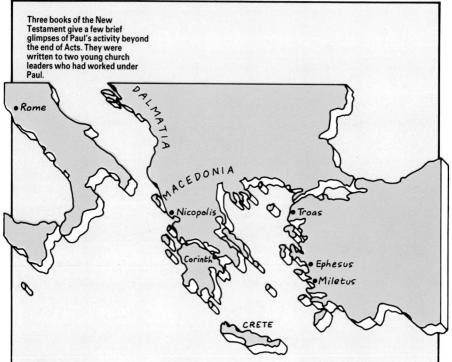

## 1 Timothy

Paul is out of prison, probably
released from his house arrest in
Rome at the end of Acts. He had
recently been in Ephesus,
heading for Macedonia. He left
Timothy in Ephesus to continue
his work (1 Timothy 1:3).

## Titus

In this letter, Paul is also out of
prison. It seems that he had
travelled to Crete with Titus. He
knows the situation there well, so
he may have been on Crete for
some time. He left Titus there and
now asks him to meet up at
Nicopolis, where he intends to
spend the winter (Titus 3:12).
Nicopolis is on the route from
Crete to Dalmatia. As 2 Timothy
4:10 says Titus later went to
Dalmatia, did Paul and Titus meet
as agreed, before Titus continued
his journey?

## 2 Timothy

Paul writes from prison in Rome,
having been re-arrested. He has
already had one trial (2 Timothy
4:16–17) and seems to expect
execution soon. But he had been
travelling recently. He had left his
cloak and some books at Troas (2
Timothy 4:13). He had also been
in Miletus and Corinth, leaving
friends at those places (2 Timothy
4:20).

There is also a hint that he may
have been to Ephesus (2 Timothy
4:14–15) where there had been
trouble. This seems to be Paul's
final letter.

Paul probably visited Spain too
during this period of freedom. He
had planned to do so before his
first arrest (Romans 15:24,28),
and early tradition records a visit.

# Index